Escape to Self

ALSO BY ROSIE BELL

365 Ideas to Enjoy Your Life Today

Escape to Self

Realise, Accept & Pursue What You Desire

Rosie Bell

DEDICATION

For Grace, without whom this book nor my life would be possible.

CONTENTS

INTRODUCTION

What do you desire? And I don't mean where would you like to vacation this year or what would you like to have for dinner. What do you truly desire, what is essential for you to thrive? What do you think you would regret if you looked back at your life and hadn't followed through with? Are you on a path you chose for yourself? Is your life yours? Who are you? Have you ever asked yourself these questions before?

We don't tend to think about societal convention much. Many of our actions are autopilot responses and as a result of this, civilization carries along smoothly. When someone extends their hand for a handshake, you extend yours too and follow through with it. Prior to lighting up a cigarette at the dinner table, you ask for permission from the people around you. You whisper or remain quiet at a movie theatre. We consent to these tacit regulations and they're called social conditioning. Autopilot responses and habits can be important for our survival. We can tie our shoelaces without thinking about tying the knot. We automatically look left and right before crossing the road. These responses may be important for our continued existence in society, but they do little to help us thrive as individuals. Autopilot behaviour is not the stuff that stitches joy into the seams because we didn't choose these actions; they have little to do with us. The fact that we abide by societal imperatives without giving them much thought means we can be unconsciously swayed in directions which may be incongruent with what we actually desire.

For so many, the definition of success is the one dictated by society, a one-size-fits-all dream. Do this, eat this, buy this, therefore be this. Much of life is spent on the work-to-spend treadmill: waking up from slumber and sandwiching generic activities into the middle of the day to be able to chase glad rags and fancy fare. Then, we sleep and dream about what we'd really like to be doing and how much stress we're under, but get up, go to work half asleep and repeat the same cycle. Modern life can be cruel to our wellbeing and sanity. It's tiring having to keep up with the gadgets, the appearances and all the pleasures we're "supposed to" be crazy about. We lose sight of where we're going or even why; daily life gets in the way. For some people, the prescribed formula *does* suit them and *is* what they crave. For many others though, this is not the case. I would presume you fall into the latter category as you've made the decision to give this book a once over. This very moment, you might be fighting for something you have little appetite for.

What the world says we "should" have and what we actually desire to have may be entirely different things. We perform for phantom spectators, exerting our precious energy to dance to the beat of someone else's drum. You could be leading a fabulous life by society's standards but dying on the inside. We cling to outdated societal doctrines and rely on our flawed education that leads us along a specific tapering path. We know about Pythagoras' Theory and can recognise the logos of the Fortune 500 companies, but never are we shown how to nourish our inner harmony or personal desires. No one teaches us how to be kind to ourselves or how to be a good friend. We are not asked what type of person we'd like to be, what we need out of life or what our values are. We are to be like the other, and so we place ourselves into nice little boxes.

Inside the box, we are generally agreeable and go with the flow. Being inside the box *feels* safe but is far from it. Within its confines is a precarious place to situate ourselves as we might stay there so long that we lose sight of anything outside its walls, and lose faith in our ability to clamour our way out. Buying into mass aspirations seems counter-intuitive, so why do we so steadfastly skip along? That would be because conformity offers us illusionary protection from judgement, labelling and disapproval. We are shielded from the danger of the unknown and the terror of failure. Breaking free from inscribed processes and behaviours is daunting as there is no roadmap to success or means of knowing if our efforts will pay off. Seemingly, going for what we actually desire is harder than settling for what we don't. In many cases, the problem is that we don't even know what we need in the first place. People can go years without even recognising that they are unhappy, without acknowledging that a problem lies somewhere, without actually knowing what makes them tick.

So what does it take for *you* to feel fulfilled and happy? Many have difficulty with the word happiness because it is so ambiguous. There are long-standing debates as to whether the pursuit of happiness is actually a worthwhile venture or not. Whatever your position may be, we all know how good or bad we feel and essentially how happy we are right now. *Are* you happy right now? Are you living according to your goals and values? Do they feel in line with your identity? Do you feel connected to your life? Do you like where you are? Did you actively choose to be there? Would you choose to be there again tomorrow if given the choice? Do you get the feeling you're settling? Are you living the life your soul needs to live? If your responses to these questions are negative, read on.

Why me and why you?
This lifestyle book is written for anyone who feels stuck as if your life is not yours. I myself was in this category for many years. The rampant societal diseases of anxiety, depression, stress and fear have at one point all been my close companions. My twenties were a tumultuous period categorised by failure, loss, heartache and separation. I had been living in London for over a decade coasting along and doing all the things I was "supposed to" do. It is said that we spend about 80 per cent of our lives on autopilot (Bashford, 2017). Now, is that terrifying or what? Things were feeling pre-packaged, we were all entranced by work and busyness. I felt restless and sad but I couldn't put my finger on why. Something was missing. I felt terribly trapped and ached to feel alive and connected again. In order to remedy my malaise I did what we all did; taking vacations, going to the gym, hyper-socialising and working even harder. There had to be something more out there for me. While I was certain this wasn't it, I didn't really know what I desired and

without any real desires of my own, I may as well have been living anybody's life. I had gotten so comfortable being uncomfortable and it was only when my disquiet reached fever pitch that I was compelled to seek answers. The blueprint that was passed down to me on how to live my life had nearly killed me, now it was of utmost importance to create my own. I was going to veer off the beaten path, to a place that frightened me. I no longer wished to rely on borrowed wisdom though. My negative experiences energised my desire to find a way out. I embarked on an adventure, which I have now committed to print, a process that has been particularly cathartic for me. It became painfully clear that all along I had very much been settling for a second best life, living on pause. I had been obeying all the rules, though they didn't really agree with me.

This book is the culmination of my learning; a declaration and promise to myself to live the life I truly desire, and an invitation for you to do the same. It is a love letter written by the heart to the mind. It stands to provide words and chapters for you to lean on as you embrace your own truth so your suffering doesn't last as long as mine did. It is not a guide on how to become the next Bill Gates, but rather how to get on a path towards a richer existence, a life you can be proud of. It is about feeling vitalised and liking your life, being alive and not simply existing. It is about lifestyle design and matching your external environment and experiences with your internal desires and needs. More than anything it is about self-love and happiness. Part and parcel of happiness is living in congruence with who you are and what you truly believe in. The topic of happiness has long been a fascinating research area for me. To write *Escape to Self*, I have drawn on years worth of examinations within the scope of positive psychology, personal experience, as well conversations with philosophers, mystics, entrepreneurs, dreamers, family and friends. Unbeknown to them, they have informed this offering which I have been silently collating for many years. Worry not, however, dear folk, to protect your identities, your names have been muddied. This account is profoundly personal yet applicable to show you how you can learn from the varying facets of your life. Your relationships, the time you spend alone, the stories you tell, the ideas you have about yourself, your successes and your failures are compass points with rich information to navigate you along the right path: *your* path. By sharing my story with you I hope you'll be struck with inspiration and perhaps think about yours. I am not staking a claim to the title of world's greatest expert; some of my stories will resonate with you and some will not. The human experience is highly personal, which is precisely the premise of this book. You are free to discover and pursue your own personal desires because you aren't a cookie-cutter replica of the person next to you. What I have attempted to forge is a framework, an understanding that we are indeed tacitly controlled. I seek to demonstrate that there very much is a box of collective desires and that living within it is not where we are best situated.

What you're in for

There are three parts to this book and they guide you towards first realising, then accepting and finally pursuing what you truly desire. Part One "Realise" is where we take the temperature of our portfolios because before we go on any spending sprees it makes sense to first check what we've got in the bank, right? The six chapters within this section detail the revelations I uncovered when I used my experiences as my teacher and explored the different areas of my life. I realised that living my best life would entail spending time with people that made me feel good, work that was fulfilling and situating myself in a physical environment that lit my flames. In order to ascertain these things, it made perfect sense to be aware of what the opposite felt like. I needed to know what it was to be with bad friends, recognise places that didn't make me feel alive and do work that was draining. In other words, knowing what I don't appreciate would help me discover what I indeed value. Chapter One, "The things that we are 'supposed to' do and want", unpicks the control systems we are encouraged to buy into and the predetermined answers we've been given to our life's questions. Here we learn how to turn down the volume of societal pressure and unsolicited opinions. Chapter Two, "The things that we learn from failure", outlines a series of missteps that lead me to where I am today, an altogether more liberated place. It delves into the benefits of failure and the bounty of personal intelligence it springs onto us.

Rejection and loss are covered in Chapter Three. I divulge two excruciating instances that called everything I believed into question and changed the course of my life permanently. I discuss coping mechanisms for those doomsday scenarios which more than anything, unveil our staying power and resilience. Chapter Four looks at the people we find a home in and why. Friendship types and group dynamics are probed as well as the pools of knowledge that romantic and platonic relationships provide us with. In this chapter, we find that the people we surround ourselves with speak volumes about the traits we value and we get to think about our ways of being with others. My favourite pastime, travel, is then the topic at hand in Chapter Five. In "The things that we learn when we travel", I recite the myriad of beautiful experiences I enjoyed when I removed myself from my everyday setting and signed up for the travel curriculum. Many of my greatest personal discoveries were revealed to me on a solo adventure halfway across the world. The opening of the mind and the spirit that travel enables helps us put our "real lives" back home into perspective. My expedition was such a clarifying tonic for me, and a reminder to all that nothing can substitute experience. The final chapter of Part One, "The things that we tell ourselves about our lives", is a note to be mindful of the stories we tell ourselves about our lives, as these stories have a tremendous capacity to change our world experience and keep us stuck. We live our lives according to many biases, but these stories may indeed be refreshed, no matter how far along in the plot they are. By the end of this part, you would have been presented with ideas about the various crevices of your life and the wisdom that can be drawn from each one. With this information, you are better situated to outline your personal goals and wishes. Achieving your goals requires actually knowing which direction you would like to take, otherwise, you're heading out with a broken compass that won't get you very far at all. Filling your life with your desires requires knowing about them in the first place.

Part two, "Accept", is where we come to terms with the realisations we have made from our various compartments, however pretty or gruesome they may be. The metaphorical thermometer you used during your audit may have gotten you hot under the collar with some less than favourable discoveries, but acceptance means taking the bad that comes with the good. Chapter Seven, "The things we gain when we embrace change", proposes that our suffering reduces significantly when we accept both the planned and unplanned changes that life throws at us. I argue the case for befriending change as a major stepping-stone to getting unstuck and enjoying life more. Chapter Eight, "The things that we gain when we accept ourselves", introduces the necessary concept of self-love, which is at the cornerstone of treating ourselves well and honouring ourselves. Accepting ourselves means accepting our emotions, which in turn grants us the freedom to be who and how we choose. When you accept that you are unique, you also accept that you have your own personal criteria and can therefore no longer benchmark yourself against external targets of other people's making.

In the third and final part, "Pursue", we figure out how then to put everything we have realised and accepted into practice. Chapter Nine, "The things that set us free", puts forward 13 best practices for living according to your truth. I commence by emphasising the importance of engaging in self-reflective practices. By asking yourself questions, you can get to the bottom of things and examine what's right and what's wrong. Only then can you give your life an overhaul. I also discuss the importance of differentiating between our needs and our wants. Because many of us define ourselves through our consumption identity, we think we "need" certain things to survive when really we'd just like to have them. Many of the things we want bring us zero satisfaction in the long run, but the things we need are essential to our very being. They are where the magic happens. Other freedom-enhancing behaviours in the list include doing more of what we like and less of what we don't, worrying less and shifting from a scarcity mindset to an abundance mentality. These 13 strategies are food for thought which you may use so you can get on with the business of living your best life. At the end of it all, I will talk to you about the things only you can decide for yourself because only you know how it feels to love what you love. Chapter Ten rounds things off with an approach that safeguards you against benchmarking against others and helps to chart your direction meaningfully.

Nothing in these pages is hard to implement. Each time you see the word *should* it will be within inverted commas, as it is my unfaltering belief that there is nothing we "should" have to do in this life. I offer no hard and fast rules. If I were to impose behaviours on you, I'd be no better than "the man" herding us along. These are merely suggestions and tools that you might like to utilise for designing your life's project. If any of these inscriptions come across as overly stern, it is because my aim is to shake you and wake you. *Escape to Self* is an ode to free will that tells you to go against the cultural grain if that's the way you wish to go. I hope this book helps you fine-tune your desires to be able to pinpoint what it takes for *you* to feel proud of your life and take pleasure in it. Pleasure is the food of the soul, and nothing is more pleasurable than being able to say you lived your life the way *you* needed to.

1

Part One

Realise

CHAPTER ONE
THE THINGS THAT WE ARE "SUPPOSED TO" DO & WANT

Ever felt like you're lagging behind somehow because you're not doing what you're "supposed to" be doing? This chapter deals with one of the most dangerous and damning words in your vocabulary: "should". I "should" probably go because so and so will be upset if I don't. I "should" probably get a real job in an office. I "should" have been further in my career by now. I "should" probably settle down and think about buying a house/ starting a family/ setting up a retirement fund/ some other super serious sign of maturity, since I have now turned (insert your scary age here).

Many of us are guilty of boxed thinking whereby there is an accepted notion of what our lives "should" look, feel and taste like, a notion which we follow blindly without question. You could also call this "the yellow brick road". The lines were dotted and paved long before we came along, and we wouldn't dream of veering off course. When we are plagued by boxed thinking, our actions are dictated by how things are "supposed to" be as opposed to how *we* need them to be. It means we are looking outside of ourselves, viewing our lives relative to the lives of others and paying heed to things that may be incongruent with what *we* covet.

<u>You "should" because you're "supposed to"</u>
To an extent, the society we live in *does* offer stipulations that we are encouraged to meet at different stages of our

lives; there are age-based predictable stages. You may not even be aware of them; the inferences are often very subtle and tend to pop up around certain age milestones - 20, 30, and 40. For example, you may feel the pinches if you're 20 and are yet to have your first kiss, if you're 30 and have never held down a stable (office) job, if you're 40 and just bought your first motorbike. Your life "should" follow a nice linear path: progress from high school to university, to work, to family and 2.5 kids, and then retire quietly without burdening said 2.5 children too excessively. Over the course of your life, you will garner respect and adulation by having possessions and earning money. The purpose of your existence is for your Dollars, Pounds, Euros and Yen to swell, gaining title after title, appeasing your ego by conquering others and conquering the market.

You may not think you are being controlled at all; you are far too smart for that, right? You really *do* want that promotion and just bursting for the chance to work those extra hours for the same pay. You really *do* want to work over the weekend as well. You really want that. The recognition is all you need. People rarely question their ovine desires. You might not have thought about this until this very moment, but have you ever asked yourself *why* you want what you want? Prodding yourself to see where these instincts stem from might just teach you a thing or two.

At one point or another, you may have come across one of those amusingly stern lists along the lines of "30 things to do before you're 30". At the time of Kate Middleton's engagement to Prince William, one such list was published in a national British newspaper. We were all to be held to the Duchess of Cambridge's standards (women in particular). She had volunteered in South America before now committing to a relationship, at which point her "real" life could finally begin. Little behavioural suggestions are sprinkled all around, whether we actively realise this not. But why precisely "should" you have to do anything before the age of 30? Presumably, 60 days later give or take and you'd be expired, a mouldy fruit and of no use to society. I personally detest these futile and scaremongering lists, created to invite obedience and make us (even more) preoccupied with age.

The fairer sex is regularly subjected to inquests regarding marriage and procreation. "Where is your husband?" asked a fellow wedding guest at the nuptials of my high school friend Stephanie. She went straight in for the kill. She hadn't even asked whether or not I had one, because of course I did. A respectable lady "should" have a husband. I forgot we weren't in 1907 anymore. I broke the crushing news to her; I was solely confined to my own company and even worse, I didn't have any offspring either - she had three children. The news left her shaken and stirred. She pitied me and offered to pray for me to find one. She said she really wanted to help me. At no point during the exchange was I consulted about my personal preference in the matter. Because I am a woman and because I have an oven, I "should" bake something in it. The life that this lovely wedding guest projected onto me, was *her* dream life, not mine. This is not to say that marriage and children are encumbrances; they are only such if they are not part of *your* vision for *your* future. Nobody's ideals are better than anyone else's, but yours are much better suited to *you* than mine are - and vice versa.

Living out someone else's dreams will never fulfil yours; it's a nightmare in the making. Being who people want you to be (or who you *think* they want you to be) ultimately serves nobody, certainly not little old you. Living by someone else's definition of success means running nowhere fast. The guy packing it all in, buckling up and going backpacking on a one-way ticket, think he's immature? He's chasing fun when he "should" be chasing success. But perhaps success for him *is* doing just that. He's painted his very own picture of what happiness, achievement and wellbeing look and feel like. He's jetting towards his best life. If we do not define success on our own terms, society will happily step up to the plate, meaning that we will always remain lagging behind. We will stay stuck in a cycle of want, comparison and competition, a never-ending pursuit of the next best thing, the shinier toy. Contentment will elude us without cease. So, what does success mean to *you*? Success to you may mean climbing all the way to the top of that career ladder or becoming a member of the board within x amount of years. Follow through if that's your dream. Your passion will be clear for all to see and most probably, you'll get there because that's precisely where *you* really hanker to be. If that isn't what success means to you, that's also totally golden. Having a corner office isn't the be all and end all of everything to everyone.

It is my personal belief that we'd all be better off if we did away with the word "should" altogether. This single word is ever so confining, further serving to program us towards certain behaviours and ideologies. Something else that we seemingly "should" be doing is being busy all the time. Busyness has been glorified to the point where the more you multitask, the more hours you clock at the office, the fewer holidays you take and the less shut-eye you manage to steal, the higher your professional and social credibility gets. Nowhere have I seen this in full effect as I did in New York. The rat race there is an omnipresent force. Manhattanites brag vigorously about how many hours they work. A doctor friend there told me how his colleagues boast about excessive working hours because this inherently implies ambition and therefore a greater likelihood of being successful. This, in turn, means that more people will want to know you. Those with the greatest earning potential down the road possess greater friend capital and only humans of value are let in. Even those few precious hours away from work are not to be wasted; you can work even more – on yourself. You can improve the way your life looks from the outside, you can get today's much-desired hard body (that's what 24-hour gyms are for), and you can do hot yoga and work on your spiritual success, leave no stone unturned. City streets are carbon copies of banks, shops, eateries, bars and gyms - to be used in that order. Here you are, get some money out and do your retail therapy (you need to look and smell like success after all). Shopping makes you hungry so head to a restaurant to refuel. Then, hit up a bar with friends to fulfil your social quota of the week. There's still some time for a workout though cause you've got to look good to get ahead at your job. Don't worry; the gym's still open. There's always something you're "supposed to" be doing. You're always "supposed to" be doing *something*. We are to be efficient life machines, bursting with social engagements and a blocked out diary for the foreseeable future: 65 years in fact. There are innumerable accounts of people working themselves to the bone, prolonging living until retirement, only to die a few months later. While you're still at it though, don't forget to keep an eye and ear out for the newest hip restaurants and bars, what's trending online, current slangs and what the new must-have "in" item is. Do spend eight hours in a queue in order to be the first to get your hands on the said item though you know there'll be a new model in eight months, and you'll be back doing the same thing all over again. Also, the more unread emails you have burning up your inbox, the better.

Modern life takes our dreams and gives us jobs in exchange. Right from the cradle, your goal is clear: you "should" at the very least want to be successful. People who do not actively pursue success are abnormal and lazy, losers even. The dire need for success is even pushing us towards performance-enhancing drugs and stimulants. Doping is no longer for athletes; it's for executives, stay-at-home mums and high school students. The trials and exams we are offered throughout life indicate that success is not merely about attaining knowledge, but *proving* what knowledge we have. The world is geared towards "success", but whose definition is it? Some people work themselves until they are threadbare, giving all their juices to the office and then coming back home with nothing but exhaustion and irritation to offer to those they love. That is if they have time to maintain a relationship with someone given all those hours they work. It is very much possible to have life burnout, not solely from work or career, but from the overload of responsibilities, mundane repetition and striving to meet expectations. The expectation to be (or appear) perfect is driving people crazy. We forget that we don't have to be the best in this life; we can only try our best. We strive to live up to impossible standards - impossible because they do not belong to us. We might make it, but chances are we'll get broken along the way. Truthfully, adhering to societal doctrines no longer has the same pay off it once did. Getting a first-class honours degree doesn't guarantee a great job when you graduate - or any job for that matter. Who really benefits from you living someone else's life? What are you gaining, or more importantly, what are you missing out on? Why remain enslaved by someone else's ludicrous fantasies or bow down to some capitalist perception of what being alive means today?

We are on the receiving end of a fountain of signals regarding ambition in work, but they do not stop there. We are to aspire to own stuff; there are also prescribed consumption levels. We're "supposed to" chase happiness and obtaining "things" is one shortcut to attaining it. The lives of so many are full of material comforts, yet void of fulfilment because we don't understand why we buy what we buy. We are sold false remedies for phantom problems yet we partake simply because it's the done thing. On the same trip to New York, I accompanied a friend to go cosmetics shopping. The woman working at the counter explained all the different items we ladies are "supposed to" put on our faces in order to deal with New York City life. There were ten different creams in total. She went on to tell us about the best pre-anti ageing creams one may commence using during the teenage years. Come again, did she say *teenage* years? Anti-ageing creams are yet to be proven as effective, not to talk of *pre*-anti ageing creams for pubescent girls. Nevertheless, those rather pricey "make-believe and prevent the inevitable" ointments fly off the shelves at rapid pace. The joke is on us here though, almost as if to say, "work yourself to the bone, but fret not because there's a cream for that". There is a consumerist response to any and all of your ailments and we buy into them en masse.

Think of the lengths we go to be "unique". We choose a colour of foundation that's totally "us"; shop at independent stores or personalise our Nike's, all in the name of having something that's one-of-a-kind. We personalise very minute aspects of our lives but not the big picture. Through consumption, we strive for difference but ironically become identikit replicas of the same life. One's cool factor is seriously upped through these "items" and credibility is sought through osmosis. We live in a very competitive world where people know the price of everything but the value of very few things. Many showcase who they are through their purchases and increasingly, become consumers of ideals. We are now to consume mindfulness, meditation and wellness as if they were products. It would look terrible if you were the only one in your department that didn't join that 10K charity run next week. Better put on your one-of-a-kind Nike's and run along with everyone else.

We work to gain the freedom to purchase things, but we're chained. We discover the world through the media and are encouraged to be the same as the person sitting at the desk beside us. We place ourselves into neat boxes, just like everyone else, forgetting that the world needs dissimilarity. Since different skills are needed to cure different ailments, through homogeneity, we all lose out in the long run. We celebrate not the things that make us unique, but which blend us into the status quo. In order to keep up, we benchmark our lives and our achievements against other people's successes, feeding into the vicious cycle that comparison creates.

Compare and despair
Comparison is the thief of all happiness. You were perfectly satisfied with your humble wagon until you saw that your neighbour's vehicle was much bigger and NBA player worthy. Now you want a deluxe version, the newer model that's shinier and sleeker. Well, you're in luck. Your car company will let you upgrade and you'll only spend a measly two years paying it off. Deal, right?

Comparison is a duplicitous two-sided coin: you come up smelling of roses or feeling like dung depending on your position on the leader board. Even if you appear to be the victor, you'll still be pooped from trying to uphold this superior position because that's what comparing is all about. You are motivated by wanting to maintain a position that's *better* than the rest but most importantly, a desire not to be worse off, otherwise known as last-place aversion. Things that happen while we're gaining our PhD in one-upmanship include buying cars we don't need, following trends we don't believe in and looking utterly silly in the process. Masks and egos ensure that genuine contact is impossible as we strive to become and remain numero uno.

A multitude of problems arise from looking at things outside of ourselves to take our own internal temperature. When we compare our lives/ homes/ jobs/ achievements/ friends/ pets/ whatever the heck else to others, we create a mental scale of how good or bad we are in relation to them. Believing that we are the only ones that are inadequate at something can cause us to distance ourselves from people and feel ashamed. Living our lives through other people's eyes is not just a problem because it dictates what we do and whom we spend our time with, but it also influences our personas and ideas about ourselves.

We also compare our relationships with ones we deem to be couple goals. There's even an Instagram account of the same name where perma-tanned pairs lovingly gaze at one another in exotic locations while offering the obligatory deep quote on oneness. Brad Pitt and Angelina Jolie were a couple many considered to be couple goals. They managed an ever-growing brood, A-list Hollywood careers, and championed admirable humanitarian causes all the while staying decadently beautiful and committed to one another. That was of course until the alcoholism and infidelity rumours emerged and then the subsequent divorce. Idealizing other people's worlds is seldom fruitful; everyone is fighting their own battle. The ones you admire may be at the top of the food chain, but have you any idea which sacrifices they made to get there? People you think are "successful" may *seem* like they have it all and are simply living the dream, but they might be laughing all the way to the bank and stopping off at AA first. It is impossible to know what someone's life journey is all about, so why compare your train to their tram?

On Instagram, there are scores of images to be seen of tourists in Lisbon posing with the infamous Tram 28. Each photo is more enchanting than the last and you'd be forgiven for feeling slight pangs of jealousy each time you lay eyes on lustrous travel shots like these. Social Media networks are the most prolific comparison stations of our time. It's right there in your hands, all the places you haven't seen and all the parties you were never invited to. People are actually living on yachts and dining in diamonds. Wouldn't that be lovely? While sitting at your desk, you see pictures of your friends in Bora Bora and suddenly, things seem to be the wrong shade of blue on your side of the fence. Social Media users are 17 per cent more likely to express feelings of inadequacy and of not reaching their potential compared to non-users of Social Media networks (Psychologies, 2015).

Comparison doesn't only serve to cause hyper-awareness of where we fall short; it feeds envy, which is basically the least useful emotion in existence. When you look at people and look up to them, their actions, possessions and (perceived) triumphs inform the list of things you believe you're "supposed to" do. The tacit (and not so tacit) pressure to follow nice and neat timelines means that an existential crisis may be imminently forthcoming. I knew many who went through quarter-life crises in their early twenties. A grey hair was found, a knee-jerk break-up, thoughts of house buying took over, some panicked about receding hairlines, certain body parts migrating southwards and profound confusion about preferring wildly comfortable nights in over wild raucous nights out. Many felt a sudden urge to do "grown up" things, especially when everyone around them blazed the trail for doing so. I was one of such people.

I was often overcome by the feeling that I was doing something "wrong" because I always seemed to be living my life in a different time zone to those around me. I had a full-time professional career job at 21 while my friends went on gap years to South-East Asia and held inquiries into their professional desires over dozens of pints of Singha beer. Those very friends now hold steady corporate jobs while I travel the world with a single suitcase, traipsing curiously from place to place. Similarly, in my early twenties, I was in a steady, committed long-term relationship while my *amigos* fully embraced singledom. Fast forward a few years and I became one of the only ladies in my circle that wasn't en route to the altar or the homeowners association. For a long time, I second-guessed my life because it didn't fit into the pattern around me.

It's remarkably easy to question our actions and choices when we benchmark them against other people. This is especially laughable because absolutely no one person has it all figured out. We're all just filling in the blanks. Comparing yourself to outsiders actually means lowering your standards, as your individuality is diluted when you build on other people's foundations. If you take anything away from this book, let it be to stop comparing yourself with other people. I used to use an extrinsic mirror to reflect my innermost desires, an inherently flawed approach that left me longing to belong to something I don't belong to. I failed to remember that I didn't have to keep up with what everybody else was doing and I could live in my own time zone. As the old saying goes, it's not a race - it's a dance. Life isn't one big competition and there is no hard and fast timeline for your life.

There are entire species that get by just fine without ever looking over their shoulders to see what the neighbours are up to or which stage of the timeline they're at. Flowers spring audaciously stunning petals and yet never compete or compare themselves to the flora next to them. They never judge their colours positively or negatively. They simply bloom. We could all use a lesson or two in minding our own darn business.

Unsolicited opinions
Spending time with young children and the elderly, you'll notice how unscripted and unfiltered they are. They either stopped caring what the world thought about them long ago or haven't yet let the world stunt their imaginations. Their lives don't stop because of what

people think of them, why would yours? Remember this: what other people think about you is none of your business. Understanding this fact and weaving it into your life will be ever so liberating. Reducing the power that people's words have over you will help you tremendously to lead a breezier, easier life.

It's an absolute waste of time to preoccupy yourself with negative reactions to the things you say and do, or even what you wear because all the best fashion statements are always initially misunderstood and maligned. The irony of fashion is that the fashionable becomes unfashionable very quickly, so you could stay nicely tucked between the lines, but the lines inevitably shift. You may never know why you elicit certain feelings in a person so always take people's judgments of you with a pinch of salt. You can never be sure of people's motivations for the things they say to you because they don't see things as *you* are, they see things as *they* are. It could even be that someone is simply looking to validate their own life choices by offloading their opinions and advice onto you. What could make someone feel more secure about *their* life checkboxes than if *you* checked off the very same ones as them too? They get you there by shaking you to your core about some imagined chastisement or drawback until you're back on the conformity train right there with them.

Upon announcing your plans for a great big eagle tattoo along your chest and clavicle, you meet disapproval from Alan, an acquaintance of yours. "What will people say? You'll struggle to find a job after that", he cautions. Alan may in fact, secretly harbour desires of his own to get tatted up, but worries about the appropriateness at *his* job or rejection from his circle, worries which he displaces onto you. In a few weeks, you might even see this person with a suspiciously similar inking. The thing is that Alan couldn't quite put his finger on how you had the guts to boldly declare yourself as the eagle tattoo person, and therefore tried to talk you out of it by planting that seed of doubt in your mind. I noticed this first hand when I declared that I was going to leave the traditional 9-5 behind for good and start my own business a few years back. This announcement was met with contempt by many who outright told me that start-ups *always* fail and that it was a safer bet to have an employer with the promise of a cushy pension. Fast forward a few years, and these very people are plotting their own breaks from their desks and looking for start-up ideas to get tied up with. Not all advice is good advice.

When you're confident they call you arrogant. When you're timid they say you lack confidence. When you're ambitious they call you pushy. When you aren't ambitious they say you're lazy. When you're independent they call you a loner. When you're a social butterfly they say you're debauched. Tom, Dick and Harry are eagerly waiting to offer their two cents on what you are "supposed to" be doing and wanting. There are ever so many voices around us. This sea of opinions can very easily drown out the wishes and desires that belong to you. Opinions make the world go round and you will always, always encounter them. Whatever you wish to call it; constructive feedback, counterarguments, help, judgements or polite assessments, it's in our nature. People are entitled to their opinions just as much as you are entitled to disregard them. People's perception of you doesn't determine the outcome of your life, just as your perception of other people doesn't determine theirs. Trying to control what people think about you is utopian, impossible and thus futile. You can only try to manage your own feelings in relation to other people's actions and opinions. You don't owe anyone anything and they don't owe you anything either. If everyone could just tolerate each other's motives, wants and needs, that would be a great start. When people offer unsolicited opinions, kill with kindness and move along your merry way. Don't let people make less of what means a lot to you or control your messages about yourself. Don't give others monopoly over your thoughts. Nobody has the right to your mind, just as no one has the right to your body.

We know better than to listen to the governors of the status quo, overbearing acquaintances and "well-meaning" well-wishers when they tell us that doing and having more will bring happiness our way, yet we listen anyway. I can surely attest to the pleasure gained from living not according to what others *want* for you, but what you *need* for yourself. I stayed in jobs I hated, I hung out with friends I no longer cared for, I read books that were "in" simply cause of their "in-ness", I dutifully attended each baby shower, I socialised with colleagues after already extended work days. I focused not on what I needed for myself, but what I thought was expected of me. It is profoundly painful to deny your own feelings for the comfort of others. For far too long I relied on borrowed wisdom to sculpt the shape of my life. I would surely feel fulfilled if after going to my nice school, I got a job in a fabulous company and worked my way up until my boss's job was within my clutches. The inferences to complete this series were so strong that I never even knew of any alternatives. You might have heard the saying "people are smart, crowds are dumb". Why on earth do we stomach our lives fitting into some stencil mould of what *a* life "should" be, not what we need *our* lives to be?

<u>The need for external validation</u>
We strive to keep up with the Joneses due to an inherent desire to be accepted, and the external validation that we seek delivers its reports straight to the ego. Our egos love to be stroked and heaped with praise. The proverb by William James notes that the need to be appreciated is the deepest craving of human nature. Love is as crucial to life as food, water and air. It is the desire to love and to be loved that underpins all other desires. The more love we have, the more alive we feel (Holden, 2013). Wanting to fit in is one of the ways we seek to be loved, for surely others are more likely to love and accept us if they can understand us in the first place. They will surely understand us if we are like them. Then they all lived happily ever after. Just kidding.

Peeking outside ourselves to see how the way is paved is anxiety-soothing behaviour. With the awareness that we are the conductors of our own lives comes the fear that we might be steering ourselves in the wrong direction. Every decision is laden with a surplus of choices, each with its own risks. If only we could go without making the decision at all. Luckily, we can borrow the blueprints from within our immediate community. While we may not readily wish to embrace the notion that we sheepishly trot along with trends and consumerist imperatives or simply do things just because other people do, we do so because we are not detached from our egos and may feel we have a reputation to upkeep. Our reputation is what others think of us, while our character is what we perceive of ourselves. The former often ends up being a greater concern of ours because we rely on externalities for self-verification. Our whole competitive society is built around doing so, from the tests we had at school, to the dating game in love and the rat race in work.

Social comparison and conformity reduce our chances of being singled out, marked with the scarlet A and cast away as the modern day witch. Competing, however, does not help you win because in order to be satisfied with your performance you wait to be judged, for the scores to be announced. In competition, the incentive is always extrinsic. You require something other than self-verification. The less you actually care about what others think though, the happier you are because you don't depend on other people to make up your mind about things.

Following your personal journey
Perhaps easier said than done, but it's worth holding firmly the belief that there is nothing you are "supposed to" do. Don't think you "ought to" do anything because you've just turned 30 or because people you look up to

are doing it. There comes a time where it's best to conclude for yourself what encompasses a good way of living and what you think is right and just. Add enjoying *your* life to your mission statement. If your actions are not bringing harm to others, you pretty much have free rein to do whatever the heck you please. There is no standard approach to life. The world is now a more fluid place and you have never been freer to cut loose from the status quo. You may experiment with paths, which feel more aligned with your own morals, values, desires and passions. There is no right way; there is only your way. Life is much simpler than we make it. We can simplify it by answering first and foremost to ourselves.

We have more colourful lives when we accept people's differences - including our own. Don't allow there to be more cooks in your kitchen than necessary, liberate yourself from people's expectations of you. A dear friend of mine who hails from Tibet received pestering scrutiny growing up in multicultural England. Many assumed she was Chinese and thus presumed she would be acing every maths test with flying colours. Whenever she expressed her entrepreneurial ambitions, she was asked whether she'd be opening a nail shop or a convenience store. Either or. Where gender is concerned, prolonged conditioning has taught us what it means to "be a man" or "act like a lady". I have heard the punitively constricting notion that "a lady should be seen but not heard" more times than I care to recall. So why was I given a voice in the first place? Limiting gender roles have lead men to feel lesser if they're nurses and women to believe they can't be engineers. Everyone's vision of a successful life is different, but being able to live *yours* in your own way is the finest gift.

Having respect for your life means you simply cannot follow the neatly planned utopia outlined for you. You will never arrive at the final destination and if you do, it won't be unscathed. Living inauthentically every day, every week, each month, year after year will eventually have a profound emotional effect. One of my favourite quotes from *Seven Sins for a Life Worth Living*, a delicious read from Roger Housden, declares, "prohibition only encourages what it seeks to quell" (Housden, 2005, p. 15). Withholding the things *you* desire for yourself will come back and bite you in the ass. Unrealised goals and unfulfilled wishes will eat away at your self-esteem, swirling endlessly in your lungs until realised and released. Look at the things you seek, what are you motivated by? Knowledge? Power? Security? What does having "a good life" mean to *you*? Only you know the truth. Why wouldn't you aspire to live your life *your* way?

You don't have to enter the family business. You don't have to choose a field of study that will guarantee you the most money. You don't have to want to get rich. You don't have to own lots of things to be happy. You don't have to be in a relationship. You don't have to get married or have kids. You don't have to celebrate Valentine's Day. You don't have to obey all authority figures. You don't have to be religious to be a good person. You don't have to love going to the gym. There is great comfort to be found in the fact that we don't "have to" anything at all. When you create success and happiness for yourself, you create this for others too by being your optimum self. It can feel frightening to follow your own path, but the authentic person fights through their fears in order to be their best version. The first step in realising what *you* really desire is forgetting about what everybody else wants. Reduce the amount of "should dos" and replace them with what would make *you* feel more alive. Get your ducks in a row when, and how you'd like them. Balking at cultural norms that you disagree with is a defiant act of eudemonism. Societal pressures can be remarkably strong, but so can you.

CHAPTER TWO
THE THINGS THAT WE LEARN FROM FAILURE

Everyone has failed before and can attest to how debilitating it can feel. Failure is a particularly stern teacher because it offers extra credit in self-doubt and disappointment; lessons you surely never asked for. Failure is sophisticated in its punishing effect on one's self-esteem. I myself have failed quite a few times. Despite being a seasoned pro, each failure was just as scalding as the last. Being defeated once doesn't make subsequent blows any less scalding because no matter what, you "should" always be striving to be "successful". The Annual Rich List, 30 Under 30, The World's Most Powerful List: these are all codifications that reinforce the continual pursuit of "success". Society celebrates success while withholding glamour from the toil and the journey, leaving the individual thrown. This second chapter takes a slightly more personal turn and discusses the broad realm of professional setbacks and the many lessons we can take away from them.

A televised failure
If you had asked me what I hoped to be when I was 9 years old, it wasn't an astronaut or Miss Universe, it was a writer. That was what my inner child wanted. As I got older, I was encouraged to abandon this idea, because being a writer wasn't a straightforward, linear career that involved an office, set hours and a regular salary. I was "supposed to" get a real job. I began exploring other career options that would offer me the ability to be

34

creative, as well as variation and a laid-back environment. As early as 13 years of age, I already knew that I couldn't thrive in a stifling climate where it would be compulsory to put on a suit and conduct myself according to very pre-defined guidelines. The next best thing to being a writer was working in advertising.

At the time, I really loved watching *Commercial Breakdown* with Ruby Wax and found that I wholeheartedly enjoyed TV adverts. I thought working in an advertising agency would suit me nicely since I fancied myself as a bit of a wordsmith and viewed it as a splendid way to marry my love of words with a career in a creative and bustling business environment. As it turned out, working in advertising *was* a respectable career with significant growth prospects, a hyper-relaxed dress code, glitzy award ceremonies and snazzy trips abroad to David Ogilvy's chateau in France (if *Confessions of an Advertising Man* was to be believed). Above all, it offered variety.

I became the master of advertising research, finding out who the big dogs were, which agency held which accounts, and what job functions existed within each shop. I found out that I could be an account manager or a creative and have different projects on the go at any given time. I could be working on deodorant and detergent brands one moment, and bras and banks the next. I began tirelessly applying for internships with agencies all around Europe, desperate for the chance to walk their walls even for a few days. I studied adverts from Sweden and Germany in order to fully educate myself on the industry as a whole, all from the grand old age of 13. There was no denying it; I had the passion and the drive.

I applied and interviewed at some major player agencies that ran graduate employment schemes. These interviews would be my first peek into the gilded world of advertising and all its outlandishness. During the process, I was on the receiving end of many an absurd question (if you could handpick a limited number of people and create your own nation on a deserted island, what would it be called?). It seemed to be an industry of fascinating eccentrics and I loved it. That would add jovial play to each day, preventing work from feeling boring. My curiosity piqued and I wanted it all the more. I didn't want to work at any old agency though; I wanted the ones that were endowed with the greatest prestige. I would get a fabulous job at a fabulous company, work my way up and be the head of my department within five years. That was what I was "supposed to" do. I had attended a nice little private school and was expected to pursue an esteemed career; we all were. We owed it to our education to be terribly successful and reach the pinnacle of our industries. I had my eye on three of the most famous global network agencies in the world. If I could get into one of them, I'd know I had made it. Imagine my luck when straight after university, I landed a job at my number one agency of choice. My hard work finally paid off and I took my seat among the crème de la crème of adland. I had made it into this illustrious world and felt indecently fortunate. In the eyes of many, I had it all: a window desk with views over Soho, working on a prestigious account with the highest billings, free dinners and access to celebrities. My classmates were working temporary jobs here and there, and here I was with my decadently elegant job, health insurance *and* enough cash to buy nice clothes to wear at said elegant job.

My former employer shall thenceforth be referred to as "The Agency" in order to spare the blushes of certain individuals (and avoid any pesky legal action due to some of the less than favourable character depictions). The name of the company matters little in this story though. I will say, however, that they were stalwarts of media, trailblazers from whom Mad Men assuredly drew certain storyline inspiration. At The Agency, the men were mad indeed and the women were even worse. I bore witness to many peculiarities: clandestine affairs between overworked colleagues, nervous breakdowns, bullying, wage inequality (perpetuated by the women in charge) and rampant drug usage. A senior executive once reprimanded one of her lackeys for complaining about being fatigued, why hadn't he just done an energising line of coke "like we always do?" These were some of the snobbiest noses in London and the honeymoon period was brief, to say the least. I recall (not so fondly) a man wishing me luck when I told him who my boss was on my first day. Turns out he used to work for her and asked to be transferred to another team entirely after a mere 30 days.

The flowing champagne was insufficient to quell the tension that eternally loomed over us. There was always some life or death deadline or client that needed tending to. Competition was fierce. The focus of the race was seemingly insignificant; this lot wanted to be the best at *anything*. They competed with each other about how many minutes earlier they arrived at the office, how many cups of tea they made for the team per day, how many neat stories they discovered to feed to our clients and prove how much further ahead of the curve they were at the weekly catch up meetings, and also who would win the award for star of the month (aka the schmuck that spent the least time at home). I'm all for a dose of healthy rivalry here and there, but this was excessive. We were told that the more cups of tea we made for the bosses, the quicker we'd be promoted. This tea economy is yet another example of the thirst to stand out and emerge a success by any means. I showcased my hunger by asking for more responsibility than I had time to accept and gave far more of myself than the job deserved. Presenteeism was the name of the game at The Agency so I put in long hours and showed up for work even when I was mentally out of it.

The immediate team I worked with gave Oscar-worthy performances of fakery. I have honestly lost count of the number of times I walked in on them tattling about me. One of my superiors had two or three tipples too many at a Friday night post-work soirée and ended up throwing up her entire life in the lavatory. I helped hold her hair up as she chundered away to prevent overall dousing with spew (she never could hold her coke and spirits well that one). I stayed with her for what seemed like hours, comforting her and ensuring she was lubricated (with water) and eventually put her in a cab home. Come Monday, said lady failed to express even a single morsel of appreciation. Her mortification about the whole thing at fever pitch; she actually scolded me for bringing it up when I asked if she was feeling better. Allegedly, "it's unprofessional to talk about things that happened over the weekend during work hours" (especially when it involved her getting plastered).

As the most junior member of the team, I received the lion's share of hogwash tasks and general idiocy. Next on the hierarchy was Ciara, a skittish character whose ass-kissing skills could put even the most cutting-edge Dyson to shame. She was followed closely by Tida, who was ever so highly strung on coffee and whatever else. I'm not sure if that was her nature or if the job had made her that way. She'd sit there at her desk tapping away with her feet jerking furiously, unnerving me with each oscillation. Next in line was Neil, a shameless womaniser from distinguished lineage. The big Kahuna was Beth, who kept us all in line through consistent dissatisfaction and an unending catalogue of demands.

Words escape me to describe the torment I experienced at the hands of this woman. My confidence and nerves took a battering each time she yelled out my name: I never knew if this would be the time I had done something right and she was applauding me, or if I'd put my foot in it again and she was tossing actual papers in my face. This range of emotions could all materialise within minutes. I didn't know if I was coming or going. Working with her was comparable to a box of poisoned chocolates - you're never quite sure which one you'll end up with. Beth was just one of those people who are always ready to vocalise dissatisfaction. Sometimes during my presentations, she would communicate this by simply walking out of the room and never returning. She had lots of cute nicknames for me too, one being "hussy". One afternoon she decided to unburden her grievances onto me, confessing that she was upset. The reason? She had been grumbling about how much she disliked me and about my incompetence to the CEO and was severely miffed that he had defended me: "what the hell is that all about?" she said. I wasn't quite sure what to tell her on that one, she terrified me. Beth didn't like going home much either. As in many offices, there was an unspoken rule that we couldn't leave until she did, whenever that was. When she eventually decided to depart (normally around 10pm), we'd be left with three of hours' worth of tasks to sink our teeth into before 830am the next morning. I really resented this and considered it to be the equivalent of giving yourself away in a relationship, except in this relationship, I felt powerless to negotiate how much I wished to receive back without appearing non-committal, spoiled, lackadaisical or undeserving of my position.

Sleep-deprived and disillusioned, my enthusiasm waned and my passion eroded rapidly. I needed a break and booked a holiday to visit a close friend in the States. I was to head to my spiritual home and the land of Aloha, Hawaii. A few days before my holiday, a powerful undersea earthquake shook the Japanese coast, causing tsunami warnings for the Hawaiian Islands. When I learned of the news I let out a sorrowful sigh of disbelief. This was, in turn, met with laughter from my teammates.

"Oh well, I guess this means you can't go on your paradise holiday anymore, shame", Tida said caustically. Misery really does love company. As far as they were all concerned, why did I deserve a holiday if they weren't having one? They revelled in this misfortune. I was working all the hours God sent, having a devil of a time with people who didn't appreciate my efforts or my presence.

Each month the entire agency gathered for a status presentation when awards were handed out and promotions announced (I called them the indoctrination meetings). People all around me were sprinting towards job upgrades, but where was mine? Envy would creep in and pinch me in the rear. Surely I wanted a promotion, right? I spent years longing for this and it was the next logical step, the step that said I was appreciated and I was good. I wanted to get promoted because that's what I was "supposed to" get, but I didn't truly need one. I was young, impressionable and inexperienced. One of youth's great ironies is the feeling that you can do everything and nothing all at once, blessed with the ability to conquer the world and the self-doubt to stop yourself from doing so. The long hours and pressure cooker environment had gotten to me and I was miserable. My relationships suffered, as did my body. The depth of my disenchantment presented itself in the form of a series of health problems. My hair ceased to grow, my skin broke out, I lost Mother Nature's monthly "gift", gained weight and had throbbing heart palpitations to keep me constant company. I confided in Neil about my struggles with the workload. I was left questioning the merit of that

Cambridge degree of his when he brilliantly advised me to come to work *even* earlier each morning so as to better "stay on top of things". He must have missed the part where I lamented about my exhaustion.

At one point, there wasn't a single day I didn't end up in the ladies room, weeping in solitude at least once. I wasn't alone, however; we were all being pushed to the hilt. Ciara later had to be signed off for exhaustion and Tida regularly let out enraged and tearful outbursts, lamenting about her twenties passing her by as she spent night after night, weekend after weekend at her desk working to please her clients who she despised anyway. Another colleague turned grey within the year. My friend Vanessa would wave goodbye to huge clumps of her hair wilting away in the shower each day, all stress-induced. I was in turmoil and had to ask myself why I wasn't satisfied. I "should" have been ecstatic about my fate. After all, it was what I had wanted for so long and there were 5,000-odd applicants who would give their right arm to be in the very position I was taking for granted. I was so deeply entrenched in the thought that I was doing "the right thing". I "should have" been having the time of my life but I was weakened. I was plagued with an immense sense of futility while working at The Agency. I felt my efforts made no impact. I could afford (to buy) things but I was crestfallen. I was on the work-to-spend treadmill. I didn't believe in my job or my company's mission. In subtle ways, we were constantly reminded of our dispensability so I never truly felt safe. I tried and tried so hard, but I still failed. I failed to get the promotions. I failed to feel satisfied. I failed at even remotely liking where I was, so I did the only thing I could to regain security, sanity and control: I quit.

Enough was enough. Without a new job to go to or the faintest clue what to do next with my life, I quit. People told me I was crazy to leave this cushy position, but they didn't know my agony. They weren't crying my tears or feeling the pounding of my chest each time I saw Beth. The environment was so hostile that one day Ciara even spontaneously vomited outside The Agency building at the mere thought of coming in for another workday. I had to leave to free myself from shackles, to be able to breathe again, to be able to sit with myself without my mind racing towards what Beth would find to be rattled about next. The first time I just sat on a park bench on a weekday afternoon felt sinfully good, the equivalent of getting up to something naughty in a Holy building. Besides my crying buddies Vanessa and Sadie, there was nothing I would miss about that place. I certainly wouldn't be missing the clients. They were all well-paid babies whose egos prevented them from completing the simplest of tasks, wiping their own bottoms included. Corporate baloney, be gone. Quitting freed me of mounds of guilt and stress, but this was quickly replaced with a profound feeling of disappointment.

Leaving The Agency impacted me considerably. I was as directionless as a boat with no oars. I felt empty and passionless but principally, I was scared to be seen as a failure. I had no prior experience with a defeat of this magnitude; everything else I really put my back into had always worked. If it was my mission to learn a language, I did (I became fluent in Dutch within three months). If it was my mission to go somewhere, I saved the money and took the trip. If I wanted a job, it was mine. If I wanted something I got it - until I didn't. This first failure hit hard and placed a huge dent on the way I viewed myself. My jovial and witty personality had come to define me for so long that having lost my confidence so drastically, I felt detached from myself. I didn't recognise this lost person who shied away from people and dreaded speaking publically. On my leaving card, someone wrote, "goodbye to the girl who could charm anyone from 50 paces". I was unsure if this individual was talking about who I was when I first walked through those doors, or the shadow of a person I was now leaving as.

The breakdown of my advertising career could be compared to the breakdown of a marriage. Imagine you had spent years of your life invested in the idea of a certain partnership and you were fully committed to seeing it through. You felt it defined you in some way and you nurtured this relationship for many years. You couldn't believe your lucky stars when after years of watering this garden lovingly, your partner proposed marriage. You experienced ecstatic delight at attaining this aspiration, only to discover two months later that your partner was a career criminal wanted in several locations for bigamy, identity theft and numerous poisonings. This desire you harboured for so long was completely wrong for you and now you question your judgement and wonder whether you even know yourself. This marriage was my relationship with advertising. My entire identity was tied up in following that career path and my Plan A had failed so terribly. How could I even trust myself to carry out Plan B moving forward? I judged myself negatively because I deeply hated something I was certain I would love.

With all this spare time on my hands, I lay calculating my many regrets. I wished I had stood up to Beth all those times. I wished I had left long before the ravishing of my esteem and hope. Drastic as it may sound, but my advice is always to quit. Quit your job. There will always be others. You are not your job. Your job is not who you are, it's what you do. I wish I knew this back then. I am not advocating going rogue and resigning without something else lined up first as I did. After all, bills won't pay themselves, right? However, if your work is an energy vampire, leave it. The prestige, pay or position itself was never worth my health nor the relationships that fell by the wayside as I prematurely committed myself to an idea of who I "should" be and what I "ought to" do. It might sound paradoxical indeed to caution you against following those prescribed life stages: grow up, go to school, get a "good" job etc, because I did just that. The problem lies in the fact that I never questioned *why* I did that. Many of us are educated, healthy and economically comfortable, yet living lives of hushed anguish. I was desperate to regain my voice and find my way.

Much sulking and studious contemplation ensued. I couldn't let this period of being adrift seep into my future much longer. I missed how ambitious and optimistic I had once been and wasn't quite sure how to fill my tank back up again. I'm not entirely certain how I eventually did. My mother certainly played a huge role in helping me get back on my feet though. She supported me unconditionally and lent a listening ear to my whining for months on end and eventually encouraged me to go back to university. What a brilliant idea? University was a joyful place from yesteryear before adland and all its dysphoria. This could be a casual way to pause my hibernation while investigating professional pastures greener. I subsequently enrolled in a Master's program at Goldsmiths College in London where our course material straddled the disciplines of Sociology, Media and Communications beautifully. I was being introduced to captivating topics and new people who didn't care about the prestige of the accounts I worked on or how many hours I had clocked at the office. I really enjoyed sitting in a classroom with like-minded people, unpacking topics and dissecting our varied opinions. The degree was however not without its challenges. I was riddled with nerves the first time I had to stand before an audience and deliver a presentation. Hands sweaty and trembling, I froze, forgetting all my words. At moments like this, my mind darted back to Beth and I really loathed her for siphoning out my self-assurance, making way for this canyon of insecurity. I got through that presentation by means of reassuring looks and nods from my friend and presentation partner Annie, who always seemed to believe in me despite not really having much proof or reason to do so. I felt so frustrated with myself that Beth still had so much power over me and replayed those horror moments in my mind on repeat. I would eventually need to make the decision to disallow that situation (and most especially Beth) from defining me. I'd have to get it out of my system. I definitely enjoyed Grad school and made two very potent realisations while there. The first was that it wasn't advertising and marketing I despised. I still loved brands and the storytelling behind them; it was the advertising industry, the nature of the work and the type of people it attracted that I disliked. The second realisation was that I very much needed to be my own boss.

Moving on swimmingly

The prodigious marriage of this newfound dual awareness was that I would create my own brand. As a self-confessed sunshine travel obsessive, it's little wonder I chose an occupation that granted me constant and obligatory access to the beach: swimwear design. I dreamt up a Hawaiian-themed swimwear brand, drawing imagery and design elements from some beautiful days I had spent with friends on a *lanai* (balcony) in Honolulu, overlooking the mighty blue Pacific. Hawaii with its rich symbolism of escapism and fun would be perfect for this new venture, my own escape from the doom of my previous career in advertising. I sought a vocation that would be an extension of myself and wouldn't feel like work. I spent months combing my brain and concocting my business plan, sketching and sewing. Finally, I felt industrious and invigorated once more. Working on the brand gifted me with a newfound confidence in myself, as absolutely every skill I gained was self-taught from scratch. I learnt everything I needed to know on the job. As a result, I am now firmly aware that if thrown into the deep end of anything, I can thrive *and* swim (see what I did there?).

As my own boss, every decision was up to me and I thought up some snazzy ways to promote the brand. This included gallivanting through the London Underground, Baker Street and Trafalgar Square in a bright orange cut-out swimsuit alongside my equally brazen friend Aurelie. There were certainly some puzzled looks that day. There was no greater feeling than seeing photographs of women on the beach wearing garments I had painstakingly designed with my very hands. Working on my own business was highly gratifying and each year was more prosperous than the last. I was featured in the National press, got to hobnob with editors of glossy magazines, celebrities lounged in my swimsuits on the beaches of Mallorca (even Rihanna received one) and the brand was also shot for Vogue Italy. But for every gain, there was a loss: a returned item, a misplaced delivery, a customer complaint or some company plagiarising my designs. These were the peaks and troughs I had become accustomed to back at The Agency. Being my own boss did mean that every milestone reached was fully mine to enjoy, but every failure was also fully mine to wallow in.

As it turns out, owning a fashion brand very much did feel like work. I toiled for just as many long hours as I had done at The Agency, but this time everything fell on my shoulders. Through this second shot at a profession, I made some new discoveries just as I had done during my previous attempt. I knew that I still liked adverts, but disliked the ad industry with ardent fervour. Now, I knew that I sure as heck loved fashion (swimwear in particular), but I could do without the fashion industry, its snobbery and all that glorified wastage. The push and pull between relevance and irrelevance was tedious. One minute you're the toast of the town, the next you're chopped liver. These things made me question if it was really worth it.

I ran my brand for about four years and wore each and every hat that was required of a functioning clothing company: fabric sourcing, manufacturer liaison, pattern cutting, sampling, web design, networking, PR, product design, copywriting, packaging, casting models, organising events, video production, editing photos, reaching out to collaborators, customer service, blogging and order fulfilment (to name just a few). Designing anything at all was in actuality a teeny part of what I did on a daily basis. Along the lines, I noticed that the part of the job I enjoyed the most was creating content and writing articles for the brand blog. In a (very) roundabout way, I was back to my first love: writing.

Why we hate to fail
Failure is the demise of a dream, a comfortable future position where you feel satisfied and your efforts justified. We all like to feel like we're working towards something. We have less than favourable views on failure because it's tied in with productivity. We don't often go into things if there's nothing in it for us. In reality, not everything we engage in must yield fruit though. What is the point of witnessing a sunset? It has no concrete purpose yet stands as golden inspiration for the poets, the dreamers and for many of our passions. A great friendship forever punctuated due to an argument does not negate the initial friendship. Cherished moments were still shared. Worries were divided and bliss doubled.

If someone enjoys a delighting holiday but gets mugged on the last day, does that mean the entire trip was to be avoided in the first place? You might spend years building something which may be destroyed, but that doesn't mean you needn't have started building in the first place. My first brush with failure was leaving The Agency without having climbed the ladder, winning praise or securing a clearly delineated future for myself. I felt I needed those things to be the outcome of my employment there. Many view failure badly because we have expectations about a particular outcome and feel we may have frittered our time away if the output of an action is not immediately apparent. This is despite the fact that we aren't living and breathing Fordist assembly lines; we don't always have to be productive.

Your ego, in particular, is allergic to even the thought of failure. Failing makes you doubt your capabilities, question your intelligence, worry about disappointing others, feel regretful and rack your brain about what you could have done differently. It threatens your motivation and causes you to feel anger, resentment, confusion and frustration: a mixed bag. We hate to fail because we are afraid of what's on the other side of failure. How will we pick ourselves up? Where will we go from there? What other options are available to us? What if there aren't any? What does failing say about us, are we not good enough? It is actually the fear of shame that underlies failure phobia. Shame brings us rejection and separation from the people we care about so naturally, it's in our best interest to avoid such feelings. For some, the impulse to succeed is outranked by the fear of failure.

Failing can be ever so painful, ever so debilitating, ever so soul-crushing. It's a niggling reminder of our shortcomings and weaknesses but can be a reflection of our resilience and strength, if we regard it that way.

Why failure is good for you

As it goes, what doesn't kill you makes you stronger. If currently entrenched in the depths of despair brought about by yet another flop, this may feel like a far removed ideology, however, there is as much potential in your losses as there is in your wins. Bountiful blessings sometimes appear to us disguised as treacherous failures. In a roundabout way, I was lead back to my premier adolescent passion, through a series of disappointments. I had initially wanted to be a writer but cast this idea aside as it wasn't a "real career", or so I was told. The next best thing would be advertising which I perceived to be an indefectible manger for me, offering creativity and hyper-enjoyment. If I hadn't found the reality of life at The Agency so suffocating and subsequently failed so tremendously (according to my borrowed definition of success back then), I would have never gone to Grad school and realised my appetite to work for myself and be my own boss. If I hadn't founded and managed my swimwear brand, I wouldn't have had a job that raised the necessity to write marketing articles and blog posts and essentially forced me to be a writer. What I lost from my advertising dream I gained elsewhere: the freedom to redefine myself, discover new passions and realise entrepreneurial ambitions. Moving forward I would try instead to view failure as a new beginning and not as something concluding.

Simply put, failing helps us learn by teaching us what to do next time around. It gives us the tools to prevent previous roads walked from ruining our new path, coping mechanisms for the future. I have learnt that while I hope to love my work, I will never again let it be the primary focus of my life. Your job won't give you a hug when you're down and out, that's what friends and family are for. It's important to nurture those relationships just as you would aim to nurture your career. The support of my friends and family was crucial in getting over my experience at The Agency. Now work is something that *adds* to my life, not detracts from it. I will never again settle for locales that dim my spirit and deplete my happiness bank balance. I also know now never to be my boss's slave no matter what. I know to listen to my instincts. My gut told me leave but I stayed in the job far too long, reluctant to concede defeat. I take responsibility for my actions and own the mistakes I made. Back then, I blamed everyone else for my demise except myself: Beth, The Agency, even advertising as a whole. It's an accepted dictum that successful people hold themselves accountable for their failures while unsuccessful people blame others. I am the only person that can stop me. I know that now. I was excessively emotionally invested in this vision of myself as a success hence that failure was able to crack me the way it did. I identified so strongly with "succeeding" in advertising; there was no room for alterations in my sketches. I have learnt not to be so tied to ideas or stories of what life "should" be.

Through failure, I learned that I was living by other people's standards of success. I've learnt that as long as I was driven primarily by recognition from others, I would always end up pursuing paths that were discrepant with my personal happiness. Through failure, I learned that making money is not a prime motivator for me. I am OK with not having a huge salary. As it now appears, I am just as happy (if not happier) working in a less high-octane role than I would be canoodling with CEOs and bigwig executives. I am OK with working for myself, by myself in a company of one. I am OK living outside the corporate realm without a staff Christmas party to attend - I didn't particularly enjoy the schmooze fests I went to anyway. I am OK with being labelled as an outcast or as lazy for lacking the same drive and desire for "success" that others share. I am OK with people thinking I am directionless, workshy or running away because my vision is clearer now than it has ever been and I am running directly towards my dreams. I wish to be my ideal version of myself, as dreamt up by me and no one else. Through failure, I have reassessed my priorities and recognise that my current definition of success is to live my life the way I need it. I am succeeding by my own standards when my life consists of travel, discovery and freedom, none of which my previous work enabled or encouraged.

When I ran my swimwear brand I tried to be a one (super) woman show and took everything upon my own shoulders. I didn't seek help as often as I needed to. Being scared to ask for assistance means I missed out on experiencing the kindness of others. I didn't want input from anyone else as doing so suggested I was unable to complete these tasks on my own, and my ego couldn't have that. The truth is, I *was* unable to juggle it all simultaneously. Now I know it's perfectly OK to reach out to others when I need a helping hand. Failing also reminds you of how resilient you are. The human spirit has a remarkable ability to recover and flourish in the face of hardship. You won't be good as new, but you'll be different and stronger. The most successful people have often emerged as such after some tremendous loss, embarrassment or disappointment personally or professionally. It may seem an overstatement to proclaim failure as crucial, but every great visionary has failed. Having the courage required to try something new or which frightens you translates into new confidence, so you're a winner all the same. Failing at something means you had the strength to take a risk. Nike's famous tagline "Just do it" has served the brand for decades by tapping into the very idea that stepping toward your goals is scary. Taking action can be terrifying, but so is stagnancy. If you never try anything and fly under the radar making no waves at all, you are by no means protected from failure. In fact, you've already failed - at garnering crucial life experience. The things you may improve on are contained within the things you might fail at, so they veritably are worth seeking. We can leverage moments of disappointment into formulas for growth. With experience down in the trenches, you'll have more intelligence to make it out to the other side *and* keep yourself there, greater parity in the battle. We spend so much time avoiding failure rather than heralding it as the great motivator it is.

Failure is a by-product of success and one often doesn't thrive without the other. The nasty stuff exists to remind you not to forsake the good things. Your reaction to losing something gives insight into what you value and who you are. Having your courage tested is character-defining and eye-opening. Whenever I would complain to friends about what I called my series of failures, they would tell me to change the way I viewed them. How would I know which things I like now if I hadn't tried them first? I usually love sesame seeds sprinkled on just about anything, so I gave sesame ice-cream a try while at a Dubai restaurant some years back and it assaulted my taste buds in the most putrid manner. Now I know it's *the* stuff of my nightmares, it can remain firmly on my to-avoid list. We learn by trial and error, a truism that may be applied to all areas of life. I have been learning Spanish for several years now but haven't become completely fluent due in part to my reluctance to actually speak to people and make silly errors. A friend once told me that if I didn't try and make those mistakes I would never learn. I believe he was right.

Moving on from perceived failures

Failure and loss are not things that happen to other people. Working tenaciously will not necessarily offer a protective shield against failure and its ugly clutches. Failure can and *will* happen to you, and you'll be fine all the same. It matters not one iota who you are; everyone faces challenges and changes. Life is hard. There will always be something in your way, a hardship or a disappointment. It's important to know that you are not the product of what has happened to you in the past, but what you choose to become today. Let choice empower you. Life is all about choices. You do have one.

What's noteworthy is what failure can help us realise about what we yearn for and our personal desires to live a life that's truly ours. Through failing I have been able to define my own version of success and have discarded the borrowed wisdom that informed my previous notion of accomplishment. Failures left me exasperated because my personal definition of success emanated from external sources: family, "well-wishers", and the education system. I needed money and prestige fast. I needed to collect things, awards and merits that reinforced my worthiness. But I wasn't a failure at all; I simply made attempts that didn't pan out as I originally planned. It is worth taking the time to define what success means to *you*. It can be surprisingly difficult to establish your very own definition. I have now chosen my career not just based on what I would like to do on a daily basis, but the kind of lifestyle I would love. I will never ever be a morning person; so being a writer fits into how I prefer my days to look. I enjoy the freedom to make my own decisions and work where and when I wish, so I appreciate the mobility that authorship gives me. I am now a seeker of jobs that keep my purse *and* my heart full. I however needed to put my finger in different pies to know this. Failure helped me get there.

Where work is concerned, ask yourself if you are in the right job. Do you feel connected to your work, or is it a place that you just tolerate until you can leave again? What career would you love to pursue if money was not at all a factor? Find your passion and figure out how you can get paid for it. Let your job be a part who you are, not *all* of who you are. Jobs come and go. Even if you are

Mother Theresa, doing wholly fulfilling work, life is too short to spend all your time working. There's a world out there, go live a little. Listen to your instincts; constructing the life of your dreams is a matter of the heart as well as the mind. Also, remember that you don't always have to be in the pursuit of success. No amount of success is ever going to make you more worthy than you are right now. There is satisfaction in the journey and not everything is a race.

Recovering from the core-shaking experiences that we deem to be failures requires self-compassion. Cut yourself some slack. Everyone fails, doubts, cries and hopefully gets up again. Everyone experiences feelings of inadequacy in their lives. Remember that to be human is to err, to get lost, to be found, to search, to give, to take and to feel. You are not alone in failing. Every single one of us make mistakes. There is no emotion you feel that has not been felt by someone else. Don't let the fear of shame incapacitate you. Developing resilience to shame diffuses the fear of defeat. Know that you are not your circumstances. Your circumstances don't make you, but they reveal your strength and might. Keep in mind that you don't have fixed ability either. Just because you didn't know how to do something yesterday, doesn't mean you can't do it today. Healing is not an overnight process. All you can do is try. It can be tough to land on your feet after a knockback, but it is possible to fail courageously. I will never again call myself a failure. I didn't fail, I tried at something and now I'm going to try something else and keep trying at things. I will be kinder to myself because I matter, as do you.

This chapter has included several utterances of the word failure, but let's shift the focus to success for a moment. I'd like you to think about how you congratulate yourself when things do go right. Devising a success timeline is a worthwhile exercise to remind us that there *is* life after failure. What does your inner dialogue sound like when things work out? Do you congratulate yourself at all? Imagine what you would write about yourself if you were to complete your own job reference letter. Think about what you are doing now that you couldn't have done perhaps ten years ago?

For your success timeline, get a piece of paper, your laptop or wherever you write best. Chart a timeline that symbolises your life. Add your personal and work achievements. Choose any date for the start and end with the date you create it. Mark all successes you have had, no matter how big or small. These could be qualifications achieved, risks you took, jobs you got, the day you met your best friend, people you helped, training courses you took part in, knowledge attained, things you created, raising a family, promises you kept, any landmarks in your life - anything you are particularly proud of. This is a great way to remind yourself of your accomplishments *and* to take ownership of all the great things you've done in your life and in the lives of others. Revel in glee at your triumphs.

Drawing up my success timeline was a particularly beneficial exercise because my focus seemed to be firmly placed on my failures despite the fact that I have actually enjoyed some considerable success (according to my newly defined personal definition). My very close friendships are successes for me. I also view the relationship I have with my sister as a success (we are totally winning in the sister stakes). Writing a list of successes is handy for shifting focus from what we hope to do and haven't yet done, to the great things we have already accomplished.

In a nutshell, dalliances with failure have broadened my understanding of my desires, my motivators and myself. Failure muddled with me because I wasn't prepared for it and viewed it as limiting. I have danced with failure on more than one occasion and I am more robust today than I have ever been thanks to that F word. I still need to remind myself of this every now and then, however. To run towards something it helps to know what I'm running from. How will I know what I *don't* like to do if I don't experience it first? Embrace failure wholeheartedly. Celebrate it. Failing makes it very clear what is important to you, and what isn't. It is better to see failure as a beginning and not the end of something else. It's another chance. View these instances as trials rather than outright failures. While this is easier said than done, it serves you to limit lamentations about being dealt a bad hand in life. A bad hand ultimately makes you a stronger player in the game of life, and these aren't just empty words to soften the blow. Truthfully, you'd never question your technique if you won on every occasion. Realise that life is a school. Problems and difficulties are just part of the curriculum. Memories about the actual class will fade away, but the lessons you take from it can last a lifetime.

CHAPTER THREE
THE THINGS THAT WE LEARN FROM REJECTION & LOSS

In an instant, the world as you know it could change. Sometimes for the better, other times not. Life has a nettlesome habit of throwing objectionable surprises your way, with the weight of these experiences lingering over your wellbeing for months or even years. These obstacles can be so profound that they affect the way you think you can live your life. Like our good friend failure, these big bangs are powerful windows to our character and will to fight. A plethora of difficulties may be plaguing you or someone you know this very minute: bereavement, divorce, heartbreak, serious illness, redundancy or depression. We are all only ever a hair's breadth away from great misfortune. That's the painful truth, and in my short but beautiful life, I've had my fair share.

<u>Breaking up and breaking down</u>
It happened on New Year's Day. What a tremendous way to commence the year, right? "I need to talk to you", he said with his voice cold and expression pained. And just like that. The man of my dreams with whom I longed to live out the rest of my days, walked right out of my life. I hadn't seen it coming. Dumbfounded only strikes the surface of what I felt. We had rung in the New Year together just the previous evening. We feasted at a dinner party held in a trendy East-London art gallery before karaoke and much revelry and laughter. We were photographed embracing; melting into each other's every pore, scent and nook, wholly lost in each other's gaze. In

that photo, I couldn't have been happier. I guess the same couldn't be said for him. Little did I know this would be our swan song.

Ours was a love story unlike any other I had known. From the moment I laid eyes on Carl, we were indivisible. Our second date lasted 14 hours and after the third, I was whisked to the South of France to live out all my Brigitte Bardot fantasies at once. Though an Englishman, he charmed me in French as we enjoyed many a wine-fuelled tête-à-tête. Candlelit dinners, walks along the promenades and breathtaking sunsets were enjoyed with vehemence. By the end of the week, the locals of Côte d'Azur might have been able to recognise my particular brand of maniacal laughter, as he nearly split my sides with giggles. Upon our return, introductions were made with our friends and families; we were officially an item. I was officially in heaven. The French Riviera was followed by ensuing trips abroad as we made it our mission to taste the world together. He even surprised me with a weekend away to the beach for my birthday. He knew how I loved the salty air. I felt like I had a home in Carl's soul. It terrified me how well suited we were. This tall drink of water was well mannered, stimulating, hilarious and kind. The fact he was a wizard in the kitchen didn't hurt either (now I had a legitimate excuse to avoid cooking eternally). He cared about the things that were important to me and most of all, he made me feel as if I was made of gold. No other woman existed, there was only us.

A few months down the line Carl experienced some

personal struggles that included him quitting his long-time job, an ailing parent and an unsound sibling. He wanted to travel to get away and clear his head. He wanted to be free of everything from his old life. He needed to fall in love with the world again and regrettably, wasn't in love with me. He put off this tough conversation till the very last minute, though he had been aware of the doubts in his heart for months, chewing on them before committing to his decision outwardly. I was informed three days before his departure. His demeanour was so cold, I didn't recognise this person. No break-up had ever left me quite as disorientated. There is nothing laughable about having your heart trampled on. It was heartbreaking to accept that my relationship lacked the very basic vital signs. Surely, this could not be the denouement of our shared tale.

I went through the stages of grief associated with mourning. Psychology and medical students are taught the five Kübler-Ross stages of emotions that afflict people who are dying. These are denial, anger, bargaining, depression and acceptance. They rear their heads in no particular order and bring a range of other complex emotions along for the ride (Lipsenthal, 2011). My break-up was truly akin to a death: the death of the relationship itself, but I too felt like I was fading away. No matter where I was, I was never really there. I was elsewhere, wrestling with sadness, living in my head, circling above myself, gazing at the places we used to go together and reminiscing about how exultant we once felt. They were the best of times, and due to the heartache now enduringly tied to them, they were the worst of times too.

Coming down from the high of love was a feeling I abhorred. My composure was now spread out on the floor like broken glass reflecting back how hollow I felt. My faith had been tested. I stopped praying. I didn't believe there was any point to it. While our flame was still lit, I often fell to my knees saying thanksgiving prayers for this beautiful chapter of my life, asking for love's longevity. These invocations being so palpably ignored caused me to lose faith in the man upstairs entirely. I had found something I so strongly desired and asked for its continued presence in my life, all to no avail. What then what was the point of even praying at all? The colour of my sky was irrevocably altered. I was truly fortunate to have a broad emotional support network I could rely on during those times. My sister and friends deserve sainthood for the amount of mollycoddling I was afforded. I was frightened they'd grow tired of my incessant wallowing. People don't often have patience for the death of your hopes; society doesn't let you grieve over unrealised dreams. According to Brené Brown, author of *Rising Strong,* the death of our dreams is called ambiguous grief and society has little tolerance for it (Brown, 2015). Notwithstanding, only *you* have knowledge of your bygone dreams. Heartbreak calls the past into question and shatters future promises and I watched mine slip right through my fingers. One minute I was sad, the next I was apoplectic with rage. I had experienced rejection before, but nothing cut this deep.

Everything happens for a reason?
Engulfed by a blizzard of sorrow, I attempted numerous strategies for recovery. I engaged in self-reflection,

exercised, and even read books on rejection and the psychology of heartbreak. I read old messages again with a fine-tooth comb, scouring for missed warning signs. I poured my heart out to friends. I went on extended walks with my thoughts, to witness sunsets, to feel the sun's warmth and let its glistening rays melt the stress away. The thought of bumping into him horrified me. Home no longer felt as such. The rug had been pulled from under me and I was destabilised, still cheerless. All approaches to remedy the melancholy exhausted, I would embark on the ultimate means of self-care. As a last resort, I would leave the home I knew to clear my head and heal. I took a leaf right out of Carl's book and decided to find another home in the world. I needed to redress the staggering emptiness I felt, get away and refuel with the power of exploration. I decided to venture through evergreen Central and South America. Fulfilling a dream would be an adequate means to shift focus from all that sadness business and recapture hope lost. Surely this would pull me out of the depths of my torment? I had spent far too long crying over spilt milk.

Until this point in my life, the only solo travel I had ever done was getting on a plane by myself in order to meet a friend on the other side. I had never travelled without a companion, without a set destination nor plan. In fact, I'd say I had a rather unfavourable opinion of solo travel. It was for lonely people and desperados. Now I felt like one of them. I had been pushed to the extreme. Truthfully I *was* desperate - desperate to feel good again. This would be the first time I simply packed and picked up my life, bought a ticket and jetted off to the unknown.

Travelling on my own was one of the scariest things I had ever done and turned out to be one of the best decisions I ever made. New unique cultures, friendly faces and blue drinks in the whitest sand would be my tonics. The beach really is an enigma for me. It holds my senses like no other natural wonder. I witnessed unimaginable beauty in destinations that I thought only existed in Condé Nast Traveller and ways of living completely foreign to my own. My trip to Latin America was a gratifying voyage of the heart, more of which will be unpacked in Chapter 5, "The things that we learn when we travel".

Sometimes even when you lose, you win. I lost a considerable amount of time through my heartbreak and the ennui that followed as a result of it, but later gained the trip of my life. That difficult conversation with Carl set in motion a magical chain of events, wholly unforeseen. Behind every setback truly is a new opportunity. Every end is a new beginning. To reiterate, these words of comfort are not just empty proclamations to soften the blow of setbacks. We don't extract wisdom from our misfortunes solely to justify their existence at all. Sometimes, something *does* need to go from your life to make space for something else, something better. Without my injurious experience at The Agency, I wouldn't have left and subsequently developed my swimwear business, which instilled a tremendous amount of belief in my power to prevail and prosper. People usually discover their sense of purpose through adversity and restructuring. It causes us to ask some profound and uncomfortable questions. Where am I going? What is the point of it all? Who am I? What do I need out of life? Without my break-up from Carl, I would not have travelled and thus regained my love for this earth and a new outlook on my life's possibilities. Travelling for those months inserted me into a new mindset and reshaped my entire perspective of the world. Through that solo expedition, I gained an acute awareness of what makes me tick and what it is I desired. I needed to leave London and pursue a life under the palm trees, fuelled by freedom and discovery. I didn't know when, but I *would* get myself back out to paradise.

As a result of emotional turmoil, I lived out my wildest dreams. Carl's departure had a domino effect, setting my own voyage of discovery into motion as well as other subsequent life changes that emerged from that journey. It is truly my belief that some people aren't meant to be in your life forever. They pay brief visits to teach you about yourself and the very world you live in. People come and go continuously. If it's not meant to be, it won't happen. If it's meant to be, it won't pass you by as they say. If something leaves your life, it's to show you that it isn't for you. So what did I learn from losing love with Carl? I learnt that I am capable of forgiving and that beautiful moments are precious in themselves without having to last forever. Everyone endures hardship, but it can be something other than a purely negative experience. Sometimes the hardships we endure bring our best qualities to the fore. We become aware of what we are capable of conquering. Sometimes we triumph due to the very knowledge that we are able to overcome said rejections and ruptures.

Rejection is the thorny lesson we've all had to learn. Losing aspects of our lives that we love can give the self-esteem a heavyweight pounding. Some are more rejection-sensitive than others. For a great many, rejection in love conjures up tsunami-like feelings of insecurity. This particular story has featured rejection in love, but rejection takes many forms. We stand to lose anything we strive for, anything at all. This is because things aren't always within our control. With any appeal, rejection is a 50 per cent possibility. You may be rebuffed, but the potential to attain your desired outcome is worth its weight in gold, far greater than the perceived heaviness of rejection. Though the happy ending I sought with Carl never materialised, I do not regret having made the initial attempt at love. There is pride in having tried. Going for the things you desire is a notable sign of self-respect. We can reduce the negative impact rejection has on us by adjusting the way we think about it.

I have found that it's helpful to view rejection as being re-routed to something or someone more suitable for us. You could also think of rejection in terms of auditioning for a movie role. The decision is not personal and is frankly about the character the casting director envisioned in their mind. That character existed before you even walked in the door; you're competing against a fictional figment of someone's imagination. Another coping mechanism could be to simply utter, "plot twist" whenever an unexpected stumbling block presents itself. At one point or another, we will all face plot twists, setbacks or renunciations. In whatever form they are packaged, we would rather these nasties be omitted from our life stories, but they mark us only the way we let them. Happiness is about adjustment to your personal circumstances. It's how you carry the load that breaks you down, not the load itself. Rejection isn't the end of the world. Though it can feel like an attack on everything that's real and everything you crave, this too shall pass.

Loss

For around ten years, I lived in London with a woman. She was the best roommate a girl could ask for. We spent evenings watching crime dramas and days devouring the sounds of sweet music together in our kitchen. She was my biggest confidante and cheerleader. That woman was my mother. She provided me with unending comfort and unconditional love through some of the aforementioned toils I endured. It may have seemed a tad infantile to live with my mother well into my twenties, but I am thankful for that time because one day she was diagnosed with stage-four cancer and four months later, was taken from us forever.

My mother Grace was an exceptionally caring woman and her 45-year career as a nurse is emblematic of that. The first words I heard each day were "good morning my dear" as she brought me freshly squeezed grapefruit juice. "Love you" and "all my love" were her favourite phrases. My siblings and I were flooded with affection. She loved her children so dearly and she would have done anything for us. The truth is, she treated everyone with the same loving care. Her kindness was what she was most known for. I remember a trip we took to Antwerp with my best friend Sarah when I was about 15. We were crossing the road and my sister and I went ahead but my mother clung onto Sarah's hand as they crossed the road separately. She held her life as preciously as she held mine. She'd call my friends on their birthdays and sing to them and she'd also get identical Christmas presents for my friends as she did for me, so they would feel cherished and welcome in our family.

Even if she didn't have much to give us, she longed for every day to feel like Christmas and for us to feel special. She gave us presents for no reason and our home was always littered with little notes that she'd left for me. I'm so grateful that I kept almost all of them. My mother Grace took gift giving very seriously. In fact, when we learned of her diagnosis in September, the first thing she wanted to do was to go out shopping and buy Christmas presents. There was no illness that was going to stop us from receiving Christmas gifts from her. Birthdays were a series of spoils for the celebrant. The whole family would see in the day with a champagne toast at midnight followed by a jolly rendition of the happy birthday song *and* "For she's a jolly good fellow". In the morning, the celebrant would then be woken up with a host of presents and hugs. I'd always wear my most presentable pyjamas that day in preparation. Birthday cakes were often personalised with pictures of us as children. She really did grab any opportunity for a celebration. Each Valentine's Day, my sister and I were the recipients of heart-shaped pendants or coffee mugs with pink and red hearts on them. Sometimes I still can't believe I'll never receive one again. I can't believe I'll never hear her voice or hear her laugh. She had the most infectious laugh and reassuring smile. Her hugs were yet another beautiful gift we were often bestowed with, she dished them out munificently. The need to speak of her in the past tense still stings.

I have always kept a list of all the things in my life that I am grateful for. I look back and review this list every year and the point that remained unmoved at the pinnacle was always my mother. I always felt exceptionally lucky to have been blessed with a mum as generous, loving, funny, inspiring and strong as she was. She worked and fought for us to be educated, listing off our CVs to anyone who would listen. She took so much pride in exhibiting her boys and her girls, attending our graduations and cheering the loudest. Mum was the living embodiment of everlasting love. It's how I know it exists. Through her, I have experienced the kind of love that's unconditional, selfless, tasking and tiring. When I was ill, she would sit by my bedside and watch me sleep, perhaps in the hope that her presence would bring me comfort. She would make me cups of tea with lemon and honey and bring me a hot water bottle. To her, I would forever be her baby. She'd even try to tuck me into bed which I found highly irksome at the time. Today, I'd give anything for her to do that just once more. I'd give anything to hear her repeat those same stories she told over and over. How I wish I listened harder because she will never tell them again.

I had returned from my travels in the Americas and continued running the fashion business in London. All was not well and my mum went into hospital after being unable to eat for a number of days. Our worst fears were confirmed when we learned of her prognosis. Our family was now on a first name basis with sorrow. The doctors recommended chemotherapy to stabilise her, but her condition was terminal. I couldn't believe it. I halted all my business exploits to care for and comfort her. Upon being told she had very little time with us, she appeared to give up more and more each day. She was shutting down her busy life and became ever so quiet. She didn't have any fight left. She seemed to be at the acceptance phase of the five Kübler-Ross stages of emotions afflicting people who are dying, or maybe it was depression. She conserved the little energy she had, expending it only to lay down despondently while watching programs on TV with me. Each time I thought, "is this the last time we'll watch this together?" I wanted her to *want* to fight. I wished I could fight enough for both of us. I urged her to try radiotherapy but she had no such intentions. She was giving up, but that didn't mean I would. I emailed upwards of 200 doctors around the UK trying to get her onto any experimental trials for new medicines. Then, if medicine wasn't going to work, I at least wanted her to feel good and to spruce up her mood. I suggested she speak to a counsellor to sort through the rainbow of emotions that would have been streaming through her. I encouraged her to talk to me. I wanted her to laugh again and made it my mission to see her smile at least once each day. Mum had these stunning long wavy locks, raven and glowing. When she felt up to it, I helped her style her hair. As I stood over her, I'd weep in silence as mounds wilted away into my hands with each brush. The chemo was attacking her mane, just as the cancer was attacking everything else. "What lovely hair you have mum", I said to her. She replied coyly, "Thank you, my dear. I wish I could cut it all off and give it to you". All she didn't say was "because I don't need it anymore".

Patience was never my strong suit but caring for my mum made me realise that I have much more perseverance than I ever gave myself credit for. We are as humans, seemingly very patient with the things we find beautiful and my mother was the most precious gem of them all. Her falling ill showed me how strong I could be and also that I had actually imbibed my mother's thoughtful nature. Christmas was around the corner and I wanted to give her something truly remarkable that she'd never forget, a real bucket list ticker. I tried to contact Paul McCartney's management company to see if they could get him to record a message to cheer her up - to call her a Beatle's fan would be an understatement. She always loved Sade too, so if I could have gotten them to chat or something, that would have been phenomenal. Both avenues ran dry so I turned my attention to Buckingham Palace. Mum was a royalist and a staunch admirer of Queen Elizabeth II. That was it. I would write a letter to the Queen of England, asking her to write one back to my mum. I drafted Her Majesty a very heartfelt note stained with my teardrops, informing her of my mother's plight. To my delight, we received one back. The letter was written by Her Majesty's lady-in-waiting who noted that the Queen was saddened to hear of my mum's illness and wished her strength. I presented it to my mum on Christmas day. She cried so many tears. There she was, little old her, holding a letter addressed to her from Buckingham Palace. She was so happy, but it was bittersweet.

The notion that life is fleeting is well established within our collective consciousness though the phrase "I could die tomorrow" has been somewhat diluted by overuse. My position is that thinking one could be dead in four months is actually more frightening somehow. Particularly with a terminal illness, there's more time to forcefully accept your fate, yet so little time to come to terms with your mortality. It was just four bitterly short months for my mum to be taken from my world. There is never a convenient time for someone to die, but this felt too soon.

A few days before mum passed away, I asked her if she had any regrets in her life to which she replied that she had not one. She was satisfied with the life she had lived. She may not have lived as long as she (or we) would have liked, but she lived well. She was happy with her experiences and accomplishments. She had four children who loved her so deeply and who she cared for with every pore of her being. She also had an extended career in nursing and was remembered by all those she blessed with her warmth. She had travelled the world, enjoyed baguettes in France, drank beer in Holland (or "the land of milk and honey" as she called it), met Winnie Mandela in Namibia and now she had received a letter from Buckingham Palace. "What more could she have asked for?" she uttered. She had gotten everything she needed and had a beautiful life and aspired for us to have beautiful lives too; ones that we could be proud of, the way she was proud of hers. It is so important that when I too leave one day, I can be able to say that I lived well, as she did.

Dealing with the death of a loved one for the first time made it startlingly apparent just how fragile life is and how important it is to be alive. Being completely alive has no connection to the absence or presence of illness. You don't have to have cancer to be sick, but you and I have most probably been sick with passivity at one point or another in our lives. I have taken from this that I could no longer afford excuses. My decade-long malaise in London would be no more. My mother's parting advice was to follow my heart, and my heart was beating to the promise of elsewhere. This first brush with real loss was a kick in the teeth that forced me to wake up and move on. Fortitude was something I now so strongly felt, among many other things. My mum's passing summoned an immense array of sensations ranging from disbelief to anger. Why her? Why did she deserve this cruel fate? Why now? Losing her devastated me; gone was my dear friend and the person who loved me the most in the world. My heart has bled for her so many times. The memories of my mum, or the shock of her absence, can best be described as an uncomfortable lighting bolt, striking in places where it was wholly uninvited. One moment you feel fine and then you don't. Grief hits you at the most unexpected times like at the tea aisle of the supermarket when you see Lipton Yellow Label which takes you right back to your childhood (my mother loved her tea). Then there are some obvious moments the missing is at full force like on Mother's Day when you are resoundingly reminded that you no longer have one to celebrate. When you love someone it will always be tough when they aren't around one day. I don't want losing my mother to break me or define my life - she wouldn't want that either. I rather hope to take from the fine example she set as I navigate the world without her. Hers was the sort of charm that's rare and real; her selflessness extended as far as her dying days. One of the doctors caring for her was six months pregnant. Mum told said doctor to go home and take care of herself and her baby because she was fine, though she clearly wasn't. She had always been the rock of our family and pretty much never got sick. Her being ill was unthinkable; her being *this* ill was saddening. She hated being a patient. There really are no words to describe my mother perfectly, but for today, graceful will do. She made me the person that I am today. It didn't matter what we did, she was always proud of us children. Her nickname for me was "speedometer" and I owe large portions of my self-belief to her. I am so thankful for how she shaped my life, for giving me life and making it so beautiful while she was here. This is not a tale of grief, but a story of cross-generational friendship. More importantly, it is a polite reminder of the power of enduring love. So when you find that, hold onto it tight, appreciate it, nurture it and watch it grow, because within a moment's notice it could be gone.

Getting over traumas
The bad news is that these negative memories can never truly be erased. The good news is that the bad news ends there. The impact of negative memories can be curtailed by actively replacing them with positive ones. Surrounding yourself with good friends, fulfilling work, passions and pleasures slowly but surely reduces the

effects of unhappy traumas. In other words, bad memories can be moved to the bottom of your brain's filing cabinet, meaning they are less likely to be at the forefront of your thoughts. Healing is not an overnight process, but time heals everything. It's hard to move on from anguish and disappointment because, in order to do so, we are compelled to give ourselves time to grieve, something we often resist. Grieving seems scary; it means we are willing to accept that this particular dream is over. Nostalgia, bitterness and resentment are much more recognisable to us than grief. All the while, the fear of grieving is actually scarier than grieving itself. Not letting go of the narrative keeps the problem on repeat. There is absolutely no shame in a few tears. Feel your way through your emotions, grieve and accept them. Sometimes it hurts more to hold on than it does to let go. Believe me, I have shed oceans over my losses, but I wouldn't be cleansed of my remorse if I hadn't freed myself to feel.

Think of what it would take for *you* to get back up. For me, it has helped greatly to look to the silver linings of each and any situation. The year my mum got sick was the worst of my life, but prior to that I was lucky enough to have travelled considerably and gallivanted to some resplendent corner of the earth every single month: Paris, New York, Marbella, Cancun, Barcelona and Cornwall's St. Ives to name a few. After she left us, I was quite fragile and travelling once again helped me rebuild myself in a very strong way. The most notable silver lining from my mum's passing is that she is now free and no longer endures earthly physical and emotional pain. If you dig deep enough, there are always affirmatives to be excavated from bad situations. Caring for my mum and subsequently grieving her loss made it crystal clear which friends were prepared to stand out in the storm with me, who my *real* friends were, and who felt my pain as powerfully as if it was theirs. My friend Layla was always offering to help us cook and clean and owing to my excessive fondness of all things German, my best friend Laura took me to Munich for two days to get my mind off things. I was also touched when friends came from far and wide to attend mum's funeral. These caring gestures coming my way meant I had no choice but to detect snippets of beauty amidst the chaos. Losing mum also fortified my relationships with all my siblings; we were all we had left. We needed to stick together.

To recover from losing mum, I may draw inspiration from the things she taught me while she was alive. She proves that it is wholly possible to recover from adversity and get back to yourself, or in fact, be better. She faced a considerable amount of strife in her lifetime, even living through a civil war. She knew what it meant to be displaced, to have to abandon your home, your family and peace of mind in search of new uncertainty. Despite these tribulations, she always had the strength to be encouraging of others. She had this extraordinary ability to see the good in every person and situation - and she wasn't just putting it on either. She really did believe this. She was grateful for all she had and took the bad with the good. If I can take anything from her, this will be it.

Your strongest armour in the battle against heartbreak

will be gratitude and hope. When a train goes through a dark tunnel, you have faith that the driver steers it back into the light. You don't get off there and then, do you? When the DJ plays a song you don't like, you wait until the next song. You don't leave the club and swear you'll never dance again due to this one perceived betrayal. Think of life as the DJ and tell yourself that a better song is coming up soon. Life is about putting yourself out there, striving, using your heart, pouring out your soul and rising, as well as falling. My unrequited love for Carl and the loss of my beloved mother are two of the most challenging hardships I have faced to date. Notwithstanding, I decided to keep on and to do the things that bring me joy. My life is to be spent laughing and gleeful and I cannot concede to all the detriments sandwiched between. Sadness and anger can't win, hope will.

When you lose something or someone, your world changes and you'll be required to make space for new things, people or places. You may even need to accommodate a different version of yourself. I had always been the baby of the house but without my mum around, I was forced to grow up. No one was coming to tuck me in now. I *had to* grow a thicker skin. This is not necessarily a bad thing: it's a big bad world out there as we all know far too well. It is also heartening to know that life events, even unpleasant ones, make us much more curious, complex people. We learn from our mistakes and memories. Between someone who has never had to claw through the pain of renunciation and someone that's racked up a few battle wounds, I'd walk alongside the latter any day. I'll always remember a man I met in Nicaragua who agonised for three hours over which selfie to post onto his personal Instagram account. That was his primary worry of the day. The greatest tragedy that could befall him was having insufficient likes on an Instagram photo. The two of us had very little to talk about that day or ever. *Seven Sins for a Life Worth Living* by Roger Housden presents a particularly interesting perspective on suffering, describing it as a profound tour de force in forging character and a great purifier that comes unbidden anyway. Bad stuff comes knocking on all of our doors whether we ask for it or not. Why then, he asks, would we choose to make a career of it? Thinking about the last time you were full of joy, you probably didn't question yourself as to why you felt so good, and whether or not you were doing the right thing. We often extend our own suffering far longer than we need to, preoccupying our minds with our failures, jobs we didn't get or people that disappointed us.

Rejection and loss are words we're all too familiar with yet passionately detest. Whether a break-up that took your breath away or someone prematurely ripped from your clutches, it is within your power to write your own brave ending. It matters not where the hurt comes from; hardships can be utilised to discover how strong you are and your true resilience. Losing stings wickedly and unabashedly, but the process is one of the greatest teachers in discovering what your life is all about.

CHAPTER FOUR
THE THINGS THAT WE LEARN FROM OUR RELATIONSHIPS

Friendship can rear its handsome face in the most unlikely of places. My friendship with Sarah, my oldest friend, owes its genesis to a bomb scare at our high school. The entire school was evacuated to the gym as a precaution while the suspicious device was investigated. New to the school and sans friends of my own, Sarah was sat close by me and extended a welcoming hand - and a piece of chocolate. While discussing teenage politics (Backstreet Boys vs. NSYNC, chocolate vs. vanilla milkshakes) we discovered we had oodles in common and were, in fact, close neighbours. After the school day when we were released (the "bomb" was an abandoned sports bag outside the school gates), Sarah called me to make sure I got home swell. That was the start of our expansive friendship. It was also at my most forlorn, grappling with grief that many dear friends made their hearts known to me. I was gifted flowers, embraces, listening ears and shoulders to cry on from some places I never expected them. These instances are a true testament to the beauty that can come out of adversity. When our friends come to our rescue, it's not so much their help that helps us as much as the knowledge that they are willing and able to. It's comforting. Friends can help you realise your personal desires as their support offers a safety net, a reminder that if all goes wrong you still have a sanctuary. We can also learn from our friendships by examining our personal contribution to the dynamic.

Friendship types and group dynamics

We've all got that one friend: the loud one, the charmer, the social butterfly or the know-it-all that speaks on end about their stuff, never pausing to check in on yours. Behaviour is a dyad or a triad, meaning that while this self-absorbed friend continuously rants on without as much as asking how you are, he or she isn't doing that on his or her own. Said person can only continue to chatter for as long as you let them. We are often unaware or unwilling to acknowledge our part in other people's behaviour. While it's easy to point fingers outwardly, another person's behaviour in a group setting is absolutely a cause-and-effect situation to which you also contribute. We may even be enabling the very dysfunctional behaviours that aggravate us. To be able to adapt your relationships, gain awareness of your strengths but also, your shortcomings, think about the people around you. In your circle of friends, acquaintances and even family, might there be a drama queen? A tyrant? A victim? What role do you play? Who do you tend to get along with? Let's unpack some groups starting with the deniers.

Individuals in the deniers group are thoroughly adept at sweeping things under the carpet. They distance themselves from traumatic experiences and avoid candid discussions like the plague. It is fair to say that my ex Carl was a member of this group; putting off having the tough conversation with me till the very last minute he could get away with it. Deniers might be the firstborn, an only child or "the strong one" of the bunch. Denial is a survival mechanism they may have adopted following a significant trauma, which they strive to disassociate themselves from (Roberts, 2017). When Carl eventually did have the break-up conversation with me, he darted back and forth between walking away from our entire past relationship and promising me the future. "You are the best thing that's ever happened to me. Maybe when I get back, we can think about getting engaged and moving in together", and "I just need to be on my own. While we've had a great relationship, something just doesn't feel right". Contradictory arguments were posed such as "is there really any such thing as *the one?*" and "when you know, you know". Ultimately, he was denying the simple fact that he did not want to be in a relationship, and particularly not with me. Dealing with a denier can be immensely frustrating unless practicing open communication is one of your strengths or you're actively willing to shake the tough questions out of someone who would rather not provide them. Carl is not solely to blame for the demise of our relationship, however. I'd always felt very secure in our union and as a result, I never called a status meeting to ensure we were both on the same page. I can't deny that.

Victims are staunch believers in the external locus of control. Nothing is ever their fault and they manipulate others with their ever-ranging emotions, swaying from tears to anger within minutes. They speak candidly about their cargo of pain with the goal to apportion blame to others for their misfortunes. The stars just never seem to be aligned in their favour. They'd manage to make you feel sorry for them being turned down for a job on the day of your father's funeral (true story). I have myself taken on the victim role in the past, but I have also afforded victims far too much airtime listening to their violins. Then there are the rescuers, who are magnets for victims. Rescuers take on other people's problems, believing that they can cure those folks' illnesses by swallowing their medication on their behalf. Contrary to the victim who exaggerates their worries, the rescuer diminishes theirs in order to focus on their external projects. Rescuers shun attention, unlike drama queens (and kings) for whom attention is their bread and butter. They exaggerate facts for attention and invest heavily in monologues with great production value with themselves as the lead actors (naturally).

On the extreme end of the scale are the tyrants and controllers. Tyrants insist that their way is the best way. They are often enamoured with the sound of their own voices and may often behave condescendingly. Such an individual may have been subject to bullying during their youth or felt they lacked control and seek to make up for this by exerting disproportionate control later in life. Controllers make use of threatening silence, glares and fear to manipulate people in their strive for obedience. They can be blatant or subtle, passive or aggressive, but either way, others will be swayed to follow their lead. Controllers are profoundly insecure, want specific outcomes and have pedantic stipulations regarding other people's behaviour. I have had one such friend.

Eradicating toxic friends
It is absolutely possible to sail through a decade-long friendship with someone only to arrive at a day when you

no longer share anything in common. An even greater tragedy may strike - you simply don't *like* them anymore. It would be tempting to hold on to this friend for dear life. After all, they were there for the big milestones, the firsts. They probably helped you in some way or another or acted as a witness to your development, so you owe them your acquaintance, right? Not at all. Removing toxic people and relationships from our repertoires can be a huge stepping-stone to securing our wellbeing. Your vibe attracts your tribe. Perhaps you have a new vibe and getting a new tribe is precisely what you need for this newer chapter of your life. Sure, there is always an element of melancholy when it comes to losing once-cherished buddies, but sometimes it is bitterly necessary to realise that certain friends take much more from you than they give. The fact you've known your best friend since kindergarten does *not* guarantee or demand lifelong friendship. For example, I shared a marvellous sisterhood with a school friend for several years. Through our early twenties, Wendy and I were inseparable and spoke to each other on the phone for hours on end (back when people still did that). This was until a sudden realisation that I felt altogether uneasy around her. The thought of seeing her filled me with dread - not an ideal sentiment for someone you would describe as a close friend.

Truth be told, Wendy was selfish, and I allowed her to carry on that way. I had never negotiated how much I needed to receive back from her. I would always go to the other side of town to meet Wendy (an hour away) rather than have her come closer to me or meet in the middle. She never asked for this, I just did it. We'd never hammered out what give and take meant for us until I eventually started to resent this self-sacrificing dynamic of my relationship with her. Wendy never offered to meet in places that were convenient for me either. I just assumed that she "should" know that it was decent to switch things up every now and then and factor my comfort into our location decisions (see how that word gets us in trouble?). People will however only treat you how you let them. I am mature enough to examine the part I played in that situation. When I eventually did suggest a more central location between both our homes for an encounter with some out of town friends, her retort erred on scabrous: "you can come or you can not come". Having things suit her became de rigueur, so this is what she came to expect. It was her way or the highway. Great friendships though are equal ones where *both* parties feel enriched. There's no point giving all of yourself away and then later feeling embittered towards the other person. Lesson learned.

My relationship with Wendy taught me a lot about the things I value. Over time, I became aware of the fact that she was a character who gained approval through disapproval. Her first response was often indifference or displeasure leaving people swaying her way to appease her (a subtle controller). She was quite a manipulative character who I witnessed puppeteer and step on the hearts of countless people en route to getting what she wanted. Having experienced the core-shaking feeling of heartbreak and loss one time too many, this didn't sit right with me. To an extent, of course, we are all put on this earth alone and it is our right to look out for number one, but I do not subscribe to a school of thought where we may barge, trample or bully our way to personal gain while intentionally stepping on others along the way. It has always been my assertion that we are all free to do as we please - as long as our actions don't hurt anyone. She was part of a close-knit group of around eight members, and she was their silent leader. If she had a disagreement with someone, they were toast and the entire group would turn their back on that poor sod. I was not a member of that crew alas, I simply watched from the sidelines. Personally, I have never been all that comfortable as a member of a large friendship group. There's always that one person that kind of rubs me up the wrong way, that I need to tiptoe around and who I cannot extricate myself from due to the tight boundary the group creates. There are also accepted group dynamics and thus, implied obedience - something I'm not very keen on. Wendy wasn't very talkative, so sometimes all it took was a look. Her brows would furrow and the group fell in line. They may have talked behind her back, but to her face, it was all choruses of "yes ma'am". No one ever probed her questionable actions, not even me.

I truly did care about Wendy and consequently was blinded by her actions and the painful truth that she didn't treat people very nicely. If your friend is amiable to you but sour to waiters, significant others or even strangers, sleep with one eye open cause it might just be your turn one day. My turn did indeed come along after Wendy moved to a new job. Of the two of us, I had always been the chatty one. I like to get the conversation going and have been known to play the role of social lubricant. Wendy was not a very good talker. At her new job, however, she made a fresh bunch of friends and a whole new set of people to puppeteer and they ate out of the palms of her hands like hungry cavemen (they were indeed mostly men). All at once, she became keenly aware of her power and seductiveness and everyone knew about it. When this newfound exuberance kicked in, it seemed like she was finally getting revenge for all those years stuck being the quiet one. In order to do so, she silenced me brutally by simply walking away halfway through our conversation at a gathering, while I was mid-sentence about a problem I faced. She had no regard for what I had to say and that hurt. The same thing happened again at another social outing. I was old news to her and she cared not one bit about hanging out with me *until* I got chatting to a rather dashing gentleman who she found attractive. Sexuality was her new ammunition to wield power. She darted towards me and asked who my new friend was while leaning in towards him and seductively blowing cigarette smoke into his face (she wasn't even a smoker). People change, but this was extreme. Trust is tremendously hard to build, and tremendously easy to lose. Sometimes it only takes one argument, one lie or one feeling. I would never be able to go back to a place where she was in my heart. I could never imagine treating someone I cared about this way and consequently said goodbye on behalf of the two of us. Real friends step up when the going gets tough and everyone else steps down. Everyone can be called a friend until they prove they aren't. It was initially disheartening to lose a friend I'd known for so long, but you can meet somebody tomorrow who has better intentions for you than someone you've known forever. Time means nothing where friendship is concerned.

Ask yourself some questions about the people in your life. Who do you actually miss when they are away? Though relationships *are* about give and take, once in a while do ask yourself "what am I getting out of this relationship?" just to make sure things are balanced. If you left this earth tomorrow, who would you regret not spending more time with? Go to that person right now and tell them how you feel and that you appreciate them. While we often think about people who haven't acted lovingly towards us, we can check in to see that we are treating other people adequately lovingly too. Do you compliment people genuinely? Do your loved ones know how you feel about them? No one teaches us the recipe for a sweet friendship. Nowhere on the school curriculum is how to love yourself or others. Make yourself accountable and try your best to treat people as you would like to be treated yourself.

Life is too short to waste your time with people who don't deserve your concern. The key is to surround yourself with people whose presence calls for your best and lights you up; people who are aligned with your values. This may sound like a no-brainer, but if you put your thinking hat on, I'm pretty sure you could come up with at least one person in your circle that you find a bit draining. So, who are your energy saboteurs? My friends are one of the most crucial ingredients in the recipe of my life and it benefits me to only spend time with people

I genuinely enjoy spending time with. I won't invest my precious days on earth with those who don't have my best interests at heart because it is comforting to know that the people I am looking for are also looking for me. Lurking out there are people who know all the lyrics to my song and would love to sing along with me. You are eternally granted free rein to limit contact with default friends and any individuals who deplete your goodwill. Steal away from bad company if you so wish. Your wellbeing will thank you for it because bad relationships are exhausting. Good ones inject you with optimism and cheer. Never forget these three types of people in your life: the ones who helped you through difficult times, the ones who left you during difficult times and the ones who put you in difficult times.

Friends are our teachers

Friends are the mannequins on which we design our relationships to loving. Children kiss and embrace each other without needing to know the meaning of doing so. From childhood, my older sister Sienna has always protected me and been the foremost custodian of my heartsease. I count my blessings each day that my mum brought both of us into the world to be best friends. Our family members can of course, also be regarded as friends. I used to run to my sister lamenting about school bullies and she'd confront them on my behalf. She once warned off one notorious rascal by threatening to manually remove his eyeballs and use them as an ingredient in pepper soup (she was, of course, speaking in jest). He never bothered me again. On the following Valentine's Day, after our mum passed away, Sienna gave me a heart-shaped necklace just as my mum had always done. Coincidentally, I had gotten one for her too. Sometimes you're lucky enough where you get that rare feeling when it appears you are the same soul in different bodies. I am lucky enough to have this sort of precious relationship with several of my girlfriends as well as with my sister. In recent years we have become so close that sometimes I can genuinely read her mind. It leaves her gobsmacked each time. However, family isn't always blood. It's the people who would give anything to see you smile, who love you no matter what and choose to have you in their lives, warts and all. Family includes the one you were born with *and* the one you create for yourself.

Friends come into our lives for a season, a reason or a lifetime as my sister-in-law always says. Despite the extended duration of our friendship, Wendy was a seasonal visitor who flew in to help me fine-tune the rules of my club. She helped me clarify my standards of politeness, honesty and dependability. I would seek people who were generally and not selectively kind. I wished to surround myself with people who would be a positive force in my life and who cared about my continued development as a person. That was the sort of club I wished to belong to. My bosom buddy Layla was introduced to me by a mutual friend some years back and we became firm friends almost instantly. Shortly after our meeting, both of us lost one of our parents. I sincerely believe the reason life brought us together was to hold each other's hands during those trying times. It already feels as if we've known one other for a lifetime.

Good friends remind us that the world is a beautiful place. The most bittersweet memory can become sweet when you share it with a friend. When my friends Sonia and Jenny notice that I'm sad, they dart toward me and embrace me with both our hearts aligned. When I come to my friend Annie with my grievances, she often makes a reference to *Sex & The City* which we both laugh at and then I forget what I was upset about in the first place (or that I was even upset at all). When you share your grumbles with a friend, the anguish is diluted. Sometimes we don't quite put our finger on how we feel until we utter the words out loud. Pouring your heart out to an open, listening ear can be ever so soothing. Talking to friends is beneficial in respect to Solomon's Paradox, whereby we see solutions to other people's problems much clearer than we see our own. The truly enriching friendships are the ones within which you can share your fears as well as your dreams. Authentic camaraderie brings along with it inestimable warmth. Finding a truly great friend is a goldmine. They are our confidantes and caretakers. They believe in you when you don't even believe in yourself. They know that you're flawed and yet they still love you.

Looking at all your friendships as a whole, you'll most certainly find some similarities between your friends because birds of the same feather do flock together. If you want to know someone, look at the individuals they surround themselves with. What does your group of friends say about you? One thing I love about my friend Layla is that she gives every day the chance to be ridiculously beautiful. She does not withhold joy from herself. This is also how I like to live my life and for this reason, we are a good fit as friends. Why do you align yourself with the people you do? We are naturally attracted to those who are similar to us but even among our closest friends there will be clear distinctions - distinctions we can learn from. Why do you like the company of certain people but not others? Carl Jung of the psychodynamic school of psychology argues that everything that irritates us about others can lead to a better understanding of ourselves. For instance, if you notice you start distancing yourself from a friend once you find out that he or she is about to have a child, perhaps you're not quite ready for the gravity of parenthood in your own life. Perhaps you're debating what it will mean for your friendship. Perhaps you're thinking about the realisation of your own parenting desires. Friends can teach us a great deal about ourselves; where we are in life, what we wish for and what we place significance on. They are our mirrors. We spend the majority of our leisure time with these people, therefore, they reflect the activities we prioritise. They are a springboard for our self-exploration. Even our fair-weather friends, acquaintances and frolleagues (friend colleagues) have plenty to show us too.

Your friends can help you get to know yourself better because they see you differently than you see yourself. Over coffee and Kladdkaka, my lovely Swedish friend Freja once told me what remains the strangest thing I've heard about my personality to date. She said that when she thinks of me, her mind darts to red nail polish. If she had to assign a colour to me, it would be red; the kind with illuminating brilliance that catches the eye. I would have never thought to describe myself this way, using colour to denote the impression I make. Through my friends, I have been reminded countless times of my eternal loveliness as outlined by Robert Holden in his positivity-packed offering, *Loveability*. Our eternal loveliness is the real Unconditioned Self that is free of ego and its natural expression is loving and being lovable.

Each friend is capable of sprinkling fresh awareness into your consciousness. Each friend comes with his or her own pockets of knowledge. Through my friend Annie, I have learnt to do one thing at a time and to preoccupy myself only with things I can control. Through Vanessa, I learnt it's OK to be outwardly confident without fretting about seeming arrogant. Through Laura, I learnt that your feelings are never wrong. Through Daisy, I am reminded of the power of human will. Bebe is the proof that life goes on. Through Layla, I am reminded to always be myself, no matter how giddy or silly. Stella has never let *anything* or *anyone* define her, certainly not society. Aurelie inspires me to work that much harder. Sonia and Jenny are testament to the fact that friendship has no timeline. Chloe is my life lesson against thinking you know someone just by looking at them or hearing their story. She has had one of the most toilsome upbringings of anyone I have ever met yet possesses the softest exterior today. Chloe has taught me a considerable amount about adversity and forgiveness and her strength is truly commendable. My friends have been a strong, loving presence in my life and have markedly fortified my insight into the world and myself. I am a strong believer that good people bring out the good in people, so invite friends and lovers who are open to you and open to love.

Romantic relationships

Romances that stand the test of time tend to include two people who are friends as well as lovers. Hopefully, your partner is someone you like, at the very least, for when the clouds of passion subside, friendship remains. The Greeks had two words for love: Eros and agape. Eros is the all-consuming yearning for the other, comprised of deep passion and excitement. Agape is the love that is composed of companionship, comfort, security, mutual support and devotion. Some scoff at the mere mention of the word love, but love is greater than all of humanity. Love encourages us to pay attention to our heart's intellect. It is our most powerful pleasure. Owing to the diet of romance novels and rom-coms I grew up on, I am a staunch monogamist and a great admirer of romance and the rainbow of brightness it invites. Romance isn't the other opening the car door or picking up the check. Romance costs nothing. Romance is joint stargazing. Romance is painful laughter. Romance is lying in. Romance is patience. Romance needs no wind machine. Romance is life-saving. A life without romance would be very dull. As with my friendships, my romantic relationships have been a source of much joy in my life, but also much hurt. Loving someone is potentially handing them the keys to your demise, but hoping they'll choose not to open that door. In my life, I have had three significant romantic relationships. Given that hindsight is the best teacher, each has offered invaluable insight into my past and indeed, my present.

<u>Takeaways from the breakaways</u>

Some believe that you only get one great love in life. I beg to differ as I count my dear friends and family as my great loves too. In the romance department, I was lucky enough to have Julian, Garrett and Carl (remember him?) as loves in my life. Through relationships (particularly "failed" ones) we learn the things we desire, what we can tolerate and what's simply non-negotiable for us. It is usually only when (and if) a relationship ends that one digs introspectively, asking the big questions: why didn't it work? What could I have done differently? Shortly after a break-up, people tend to have overly catastrophic perceptions about the future of their lives, particularly if the decision to separate was sudden and not theirs. Through relationships, we collect data to adapt our boundaries, align how much of ourselves we are willing to give and who best to give ourselves to.

My first real boyfriend Julian and I had a solid relationship that contained much warmth and devotion. What it did not contain though was passion. Julian's passion was reserved for his football team. He was somehow able to power his ship on only 50 per cent battery; the glass was always ever so half empty for him. I felt he never itched for anything, not even for himself. Candles of enthusiasm were blown out swiftly in our household. He said no to everything first and like a good cheerleader, I'd talk him into things we both knew he would ultimately enjoy. His second favourite response was "I don't know". No matter what the question was, the stance he took was laissez-faire. Towards the end, it was clear neither of us were fulfilled though he probably would have kept on coasting along with me - another sign of his lack of zeal to improve his situation. Contrastingly, Julian scolded me for wanting too much out of life and declared that my standards were too high because I feverishly fantasised about finding a job that would uproot me from London and take me to the warmth - let's face it, the city isn't exactly known for its blazing summers. It isn't folly to believe that people say that your standards are too high when they want you to lower them for their convenience. Ultimately, the people who really want to be in your life will rise up to meet your standards, so don't apologise for having them or lower them to cater to those who won't raise theirs - in any kind of relationship. Julian and I needed different things and had contrasting ideas on how to paint our life portraits. We were good friends, but ours was not a love story. We both lingered around trying to cling to the good stuff leading the relationship to overrun its sell-by date by a few years, a mistake in itself. We were scared to walk away and of what life would look like minus our other half. Through Julian, I learned not to let the fear of the unknown keep me in less than ideal situations. Holding on to a fledgling relationship is a painful reminder of how good things once were. Good relationships boost your appetite to persist; bad ones deplete you.

Things got warmer with Garrett. He was an out-of-towner I met under particularly twinkly circumstances on a brisk London evening (Rachel McAdams would be proud). From beginning to end, I was swept into this enchanting dream. He even took me back to the initial spot where we met to tell me he loved me for the first time. Though I knew he would be leaving the country in a few months, I still let myself fall heart first into his embrace and his promise. Sincerely, I was enmeshed in the fantasy of being uprooted from London finally. I essentially felt I "required" someone to liberate me from my dissatisfaction with my London life. Garrett presented an amazing adventure where I would move to the U.S. to be with him, we'd drink Midwestern craft beer together, pay for everything in Dollars and live happily ever after. I wasn't a happy person in those days, nor was I reaching my potential. I was waiting for someone else to make me happy, a sure-fire way to be sad. I eagerly sought distraction from my discontent. This "requiring" meant that I largely brushed over our incompatibilities, prioritising the story of us over the reality of him. He wasn't all that keen on the pressure the situation created either as the more I'd give up for him (leaving it all behind and crossing the Atlantic to be together), the greater the pressure for a first class outcome. The moral of this tale is that boredom, distraction, escapism and loneliness are never great reasons to get into a relationship. The relationship will be nothing but a temporary fix, the equivalent of using mouthwash when what you really need is a filling.

I'd had my fill of love after my break-up with Carl. I couldn't imagine feeling this good with anyone else ever again. Carl had, in my opinion, a magical aura around him, an authentic allure, charm - and bags full of it. This captivated me and held my attention unflinchingly, more so than any man before him. The components of charm are presence, wit, warmth and self-confidence. People say yes to those bestowed with charm despite them never asking a question. That's the thing about charming people; they'd still come up smelling of roses after committing double murder. He also possessed a healthy sense of humour and was one of the most intelligent individuals I'd crossed paths with. Nevertheless, once the pain started to subside and the clouds of love that distorted my vision dispersed, I realised that he really wasn't the prodigious figure I'd imagined him to be. It totally drove me up the wall that he couldn't watch a movie if it had scored lower than 70 per cent on Rotten Tomatoes. He complained about absolutely everything we watched if I was the one who had selected it. I was dealing with a know-it-all. Carl loved feeling right even when he wasn't actually correct. He was the kind of person that would tell you with certainty where the wind would blow next and that the way you were making the recipe was wrong. Underneath it all, he was altogether quite cynical about love, despite his grandiose gestures of romance. His previous relationships had all ended amidst questionable circumstances. Anything relating to the pursuit of happiness was stomach turning to him. Therapy was for the weak and no counsellor could be good enough. He would have balked at the very idea of the books I write.

Looking back, our relationship suffered from an intimacy gap; whereby one partner wants to experience and express sincere intimacy while the other doesn't. We talked openly about absolutely everything under the sun (politics, the meaning of life, family, career), absolutely everything besides our relationship. Once I attempted to broach a difficult subject with him. I told him I wanted to open up about something fairly distressing from my past. The fact I had kept this record from him until then suggested it was serious and that things might get heavy. To diffuse the situation, he turned it into a game. When I landed at the last word of any sentence, he would play the DJ and put on a fun tune with that last word I had said in the song title. We would then have to sing along to that song and do a little dance before I'd proceed to the next part of my story. This, he said, was a strategy to keep me from tears but in actuality, it was a guise to avoid connecting on a deeper level and having that "stare into each other's eyes" moment. Carl was not prepared to accept love from me or anyone for that matter. Our break-up was an exquisitely painful lesson to in the future, seek out people who hope to be more loving people. Our pain isn't pointless. Life is trying to show us something. The function of pain is to avert trouble for you in the future, like a burn. When you stick your finger in a candle flame, it stings so you know not to play with the fire again. Maybe you know not to leave your finger in the flame too long. So you tried, maybe you just need to try differently next time. Personal growth is a process of trial-and-error that requires owning up to our blunders. I will now choose only those who are gleefully proud to occupy any space in my heart. The foremost rule of my love club is that any member cares for and about me, with an invested interest in my present and my future if they are to be in it. So many people condemn true vulnerability. I won't be one of them. Love or being in love can be a hard thing to master. We ache for love, yet fight it tempestuously. Relationships are made all the harder when we don't speak the other person's language of love.

The Five Love Languages

The Five Love Languages by Gary Chapman has sold about a gazillion copies since being first published over 25 years ago (well, more like 11 million). The book specifies that we give and receive love through five languages: touch, gifts, words of affirmation, acts of service and quality time. Chapman contends that while we all enjoy and can comprehend all five, each person has a primary language and a secondary language. The primary language can be viewed as one's mother tongue. Imagine talking to someone in French when they speak Farsi? That individual would naturally prefer you to use Farsi when approaching them, even though they may understand titbits of Français. You reaching out to them in their native tongue would bring you closer faster and soften you in their estimations. We also give love in the ways we like to receive it. It works both ways. In order to better understand the notion of *The Five Love Languages*, I shall outline three key examples from my personal experience in three relationships.

My primary and secondary languages of love are touch and gifts. The way to my heart is through both petting and presents. With the one I care for, I want to steal kisses and embraces as often as I can and nothing adds an element of revelry to my days than a gift out of the blue. I realise that my adoration of gift giving stemmed from my mother, as this was one the ways she showered us with love growing up. Gifting shows an understanding of interests or taste, and the presents needn't cost anything either. The more thoughtful and personalised, the better. Julian's love languages were acts of service and words of affirmation, meaning we spoke neither of each other's preferred dialects. Whenever I felt low, he'd remind me of my marvel and tell me I could do it (words of affirmation). He was very reliable and I always knew I could count on him to be there to pick me up from the tube station and walk me to his place, especially if it was late at night (acts of service). I felt I could depend on him when the going got tough, but I didn't feel he loved me. Instead of speaking to Julian in his languages, I spoke to him in mine, the languages I am fluent in. I would plan what to get him for his birthday months in advance: personalised football shirts, game tickets, surprise birthday parties with all his friends from far and wide (gifts). I would always take his hand when we walked and offer to give him back massages after a tough day (touch). I did those things because that's what makes *me* feel the most treasured, and I wanted him to feel treasured by me. I actively articulated what I wanted and needed from him but he was unable (and often reluctant) to reciprocate. He shunned physical contact outdoors and said kissing in front of other people "would make them feel bad about their day" and I'd think, "don't you care about making *me* feel bad right now?" Where public displays of affection were concerned (touch), he felt self-conscious while I felt rejected. He also thought it was silly how much emphasis I placed on gifts. He would consistently wait till the last minute to get me a present and often ended up giving me one long after the event. Gift giving was infantile and receiving presents was neither here nor there for him. We cared for each other, but there was a clear disconnect. The problem was not that we lacked fluency in each other's languages; it was that we weren't willing to try to gain it.

Garrett and I shared one love language in common: gifts. Shortly after we met in London, he had to return to the States. Garrett would have presents shipped to me in London all the way from Chicago. It was the ultimate gesture that said, "no matter how far away you are, I'm still thinking of you". I was so bowled over by these gifts and am wholly convinced that they contributed to me becoming enamoured of him as powerfully as I was. Postcards with declarations of his love were followed by speciality Dutch cheeses (inside joke, don't ask). It was as if all my Christmases had come at once. I was more than happy to return the favour, making him personalised cards and love notes. Garrett paid an extended visit to London to spend time with me and it was then we learned that touch was not one of his love languages. He shared Julian's aversion to PDA and also wholly opposed cuddling. He didn't enjoy back massages either. I always felt our kisses were punctuated, I could never get lost in them because he would stop before I was ready. I needed more physical interaction. I was expressing my desire for him, but he didn't seem to want it. Garrett's secondary love language is words of affirmation, similar to Julian. He loved when I'd offer encouragement about the projects he was working on and told him that I believed in him. I was able to speak both of his, but he wasn't communicating in my primary *and* secondary languages of love.

Carl spoke English and French as well as my two love languages. I felt the sun shining on both sides. Our physical closeness was unsurpassed. Most nights, we held each other ever so tightly in the hope of pretending we were, in fact, one body and not two. We'd take turns holding hands with his hand over mine and then mine over his. If our limbs weren't entangled together, then his hand was placed affectionately on the small of my back. Carl was generous in every sense of the word. He knew what drink I'd like and it was ordered before I had time to even think about it. Carl inviting me on that maiden trip to the South of France was the permission I needed to run to him at full gallop. Travel is my drug and he wasn't shy about writing prescriptions. I had everything I needed, but he didn't. Receiving gifts made Carl feel uneasy. He felt undeserving and awkward about them. His second love idiom was acts of service. He was the one all his family members leaned on. With severe illness plaguing multiple members of his family, a lot fell on his shoulders. Carl may have felt more comforted by someone he could apportion half of his burdens to, rather than somebody who'd bake him a chocolate cake when he was feeling down. My gifts weren't what he required to remedy his plight.

The Five Love Languages is sophisticated in its use of a simple tool as language to explicate the harmony and chaos in relationships where both parties do share love. Chapman has a particularly interesting perspective because we all know how stifled we feel when we're lost for words and can't communicate with the person in front of us. We know how helpless and lonely it would feel to be the only person in the room that speaks our language. Imagine if that room was your relationship. Chapman proposes that "the one who chooses to love will find appropriate ways to express that decision every day". Knowing my personal love languages, my mission is to happen upon relationships with individuals who know theirs and are willing to learn mine. Even thinking about my closest friendships, I share at least one common love language with each pal. It simply makes sense. Understanding the language that cuts through the noise and goes straight to your heart can not only help you love others better but also supplies you with the info to give yourself the gift of love. So, what's your love language? Touch, words of affirmation, acts of service, quality time or gifts?

<u>What does your heart beat for?</u>
Any kind of relationship is a piece of your life's puzzle. What landscape does the puzzle depict? If you need a life filled with passion, love, adventure, sport, art, play, kindness, or warmth, surround yourself with those very things. If you wish to run free, find someone just as wild to run with. When you think deeply about what you need out of life and who you are, you do know whether someone is an ideal companion for you or not. If you were only allowed to spend the rest of life with just ten people, would you choose the ones you're with now? If not, skedaddle your way out of there. Keep the ones that make you smile and renounce the ones that don't. It's better to keep no company than bad company. You're a free agent; you can roam if you wish to.

CHAPTER FIVE
THE THINGS THAT WE LEARN WHEN WE TRAVEL

Peripatetic: an itinerant stance whereby one moves incessantly from place to place. Nothing has shown me how much and how little I know like travel has. It's been my greatest teacher and inspiration. Different locations have acted as different tutors, imbibing me with potent lessons that I am forever marked by. Travelling has also been my greatest pleasure. I have collected my best stories on the road and it's never long before I'm taking a bite out of a new territory. I have found and lost my heart so many times - in people and in places. Travel has come to my rescue on the many occasions my soul thirsted for rejuvenation: when heartbroken, while grieving. In many cases, leaving your home finds you a new one.

<u>An adventure into the tropics</u>
After the demise of my relationship with Carl I was in search of an experience of life that excluded anguish but rather included expedition and thrill. I needed to get away to hear my own voice again and refocus my life. I bought a ticket to Costa Rica with accommodation booked for the first few days only, but little other planning. I was going to take a page out of the Hawaiians' book and go holoholo. Hawaiians say, "let's go holoholo" when embarking on a long day at the beach or blissfully cruising around the islands. Holoholo is the Hawaiian word for travelling for fun without a set destination, leisurely gallivanting, taking in life's pleasures, joy riding

and having a jolly good time. There is no set destination or aim besides leisure and pleasure. The mantra is that it's not where they plan to go, but where they end up; emphasis is placed on the journey itself. There I was, paradise bound. I was on the edge of my dream and about to jump out of my comfort zone (or discomfort zone rather).

Before I left, I was teetering on a tightrope between excitement and agonizing fear. I felt I was being both courageous and careless. I was travelling solo for the first time: what if I was lonely? What if I encountered danger? What if it was all a big mistake? What if I got homesick or bored? Specifically to prepare for the journey, I bought Roger Housden's *Seven Sins for a Life Worth Living*. It caught my eye due to one of its chapters called "The pleasure of doing nothing useful". I felt I needed this because I never knew how to do nothing in my chronically busy life in London. Years of programming had turned me into a utilitarian. Whenever I put time aside to relax or paint, I was riddled with guilt. I felt guilty that I wasn't being productive, that I was wasting time somehow. If it wasn't useful, what was the point of doing it? The book and this chapter, in particular, did a world of good and helped me ease into my newfound freedom - the freedom to gallivant, to breathe, to think, to simply be. As Housden notes, the task of the individual lies predominantly in wholeheartedly enjoying life. He specifies that "when you die, God and the angels will hold you accountable for all the pleasures you were allowed in life that you denied yourself" (Housden, 2005, p. 14). Well, I surely wouldn't want that, would I?

The first couple of days were sensory bombardment. Afternoons consisted of coastal bike rides, hikes through secret paths to uncover rewarding vistas, monkey spotting in the cloud forest, sloth sightings and finally, I made acquaintance with a keel-billed toucan; the ultimate symbol of paradise. I explored the width and breadth of Costa Rica, from the Pacific coast to its Caribbean villages. In Puerto Viejo de Talamanca I stayed in a hostel for the first time in my life and loved this multinational nomadic environment. I was once at a dinner table sitting next to a Frenchman who spoke no English, a Luxembourgian who spoke no Spanish, a German girl who spoke no French and a Costa Rican and Swiss guy who spoke no German. Somehow within this melee, we all knew the same songs which we'd get up and dance to together. Being put in this comedic situation made me come alive. I hadn't felt that way in months. None of us were from the same place. How lovely it was. Many evenings I would sit on the balcony with my eyes closed, taking in the sway of the Caribbean Sea which happened to be at the very foot of the hostel. I drank in the pleasure of doing nothing like a bottle of the finest champagne. I had no concrete plans, nowhere I needed to be - and I liked it that way. This also meant that anything could happen. The days were open to welcome any and every possibility. The old me would have been thoroughly uncomfortable with this level of uncertainty, now I was living by it. Slowly but surely, my shackles of sadness paralysis were coming undone. Every now and then, the nightmarish scenario of Carl having a new girlfriend would creep into my mind, but I couldn't let that destroy my living daydream. Here I was anonymous and free to do as I pleased. Nobody knew Carl here; this was a Carl-free zone. These places and people had absolutely zero connection to my life in London. It was delicious. I felt so lucky, so free; like my old self before the gloom took over. As time went by I thought less and less of Carl, I was high on summer time.

My family lived a somewhat nomadic lifestyle relocating to a new country more or less every five years. The first family holiday I went on was to the coastal city of Swakopmund in Namibia, where we lived. That was the beginning of a lifelong beach love affair. As a child, I thought everyone lived by the ocean, because how could one live anywhere else? I am no stranger to the beach lifestyle and have forever felt at home under the sun; it's my preferred accessory. For a sunny soul like myself, winters are particularly trying. The fewer the sunny daylight hours, the less sanguine my disposition. Nature plays a tremendous part in how we experience the world. Access to natural light helps to open up the mind and drowns out the noise; it has immense aggression-reducing properties too. The beach boosts my mind, body and lifts my spirit. So when I needed replenishment, I knew to go to the oceanfront.

Speaking of oceanfront, Panama is blessed with miles and miles of it (1,500 to be precise). During my trip, I journeyed through four countries but Panama was the one that put a smile on my heart the most. I had never planned on going to Panama but I found myself there pretty much by accident. Any traveller worth their salt knows that there are few places which remain forever emblazoned in your soul in a special way. I happened to find mine in Panama. Here was that elusive feeling of home I sought in London all those years. Panama is a country of contradictions: its capital city is utterly modern and progressive, while some of the rural areas are like a time warp back to the adventures of Robinson Crusoe: Western vibes, with Latin flavour and a pinch of the Caribbean thrown in for good measure. From the moment I stepped foot on its soil, things were kicked up a notch. I arrived in Panama City and was immediately engulfed by the beauty of my surroundings. The historic old town of Casco Viejo meets the futuristic skyscrapers of the city centre granting Panama City the moniker of "Miami of the south". The skyscrapers are evidence of the city's ambitions as are the numerous rooftop bars, too many to choose from. What better place to feel the wind in your hair than on a fabulous rooftop, caressing the clouds? Walking through Casco Viejo uncovered many cute cafes and restaurants that you'd hear the most inviting salsa music escaping out from. My travel buddies Anne and Elisa would often stop right there and then for a cheeky kerbside salsa dance. The way of life here really resonated with me.

Panama lead me by the heart to discover more of its corners. Historically, I have always gone where there is fun to be had so it's not too surprising that I found myself in Bocas del Toro. You'll often hear of places where travellers tend to get stuck (in a good way). Never had I witnessed this with my own eyes before I went to Bocas del Toro, the boisterous archipelago in the west of Panama. Between the palm-lined pathways of these nine islands, I found sweet enchantment. The novelty of actually having to take a scenic water taxi as my primary means of inter-island transport never wore off. Bocas is home to one of my favourite beaches in the world: Starfish Beach. What it lacked in waves, it made up for in abundance of gorgeous echinoderms (that's starfish to you and me) trickled all over the bottom of the ocean - I guess they don't call it Starfish Beach for nothing. It was near impossible to take a bad picture in Bocas. If you believe in the Garden of Eden, Bocas might just be it. On top of hitting the jackpot of postcard-worthiness, I happened to meet the loveliest people in Bocas too. Turns out I needn't have worried about being lonely on the trip, because Bocas attracted scores of curious souls just like me, beckoned by its sweet nectar. My first amigos on the island were Christian missionaries, Matt and Tristan. They drank like sailors and smoked Cuba's finest cigars but were fervent churchgoers and quoted Bible passages like there was no tomorrow (a nod to The Book of Revelation there). They were certainly a lesson in not putting people in boxes. I felt safe in their company and they really listened *and* heard me. I will always hold on to such people. Then there was Sam and Dave who never ever wore shoes, not even once. Anne was a pleasure to be around due to her youthful enthusiasm and Elisa possessed the most luminous smile and insatiable energy for dancing. You couldn't stop her. She was put on bed rest after having her appendix removed, but her biggest lament was being unable to shake her booty for a few days. Next come my partners in crime Jess and Fran. Like Ying and Yang, we were wholly in sync. They let me be me and never judged me no matter how featherbrained my behaviour was. Most likely they were right there beside me being just as silly, talking to the meat stick man at daybreak outside *La Iguana* bar after yet another raucous ladies night.

One of my most moving memories was of an early evening at our favourite surf lounge taking in an acoustic performance from Isaac, one of the diving instructors. Sitting with Jess, Anne and Elisa taking in his raspy voice and Spanish guitar during the blue hour was magical. I felt like I was melting into my chair and shed a single tear of joy. This is how good life could feel, full of beautiful moments that take your breath away. I was where I longed to be and with whom. I loved my Panamanian life. A little sand between the toes really did help to take away my woes. Once my trip was over and I returned to London, I had shaken the sand off my clothes, but it never left my spirit.

Travel as an education
There is no concrete curriculum when you travel, only the one you choose to follow. So much can be learnt from travel besides the obvious. First and foremost, it became clear to me the benefits that may be reaped from openness and positivity. Today I wholeheartedly believe in energies. Because I was open and saying yes to life, great experiences came my way without as much as trying. This is not to say everything was honky dory smooth sailing by any means. I was hit with bronchitis in Nicaragua and had to see the only doctor in the village who spoke very little English and back then I spoke just enough Spanish to understand Daddy Yankee's *Gasolina*.

Also, en route to Colombia, I was running late for my flight and forgot to put some warm clothing in my hand luggage. Shivering and desperate, I asked the one person in front of me if he had any spare items of clothing I could borrow. He didn't have any on his person but offered me a towel, which I very happily accepted. It didn't quite match my impractical but cute crop top and sun hat combo, but on the brink of hypothermia, this towel was essentially manna from heaven. The lovely towel-wielding gentleman and I ended up having a great chat about life, love and gratitude on the flight. He gave me his card and we have maintained a warm friendship till today. A great companion came into my life because we were both open.

My second realisation from my voyage of discovery was that I am less constrained when visiting somewhere outside of my normative environment (I know what you're thinking - aren't we all?). I cared less about "the rules" I'd been taught back home. I shall illustrate this point with the topics of lip-syncing and singing. In London, it is highly frowned-upon to make eye contact with other passengers on public transport. Just keep your head down and mind your own business. Don't get in anyone's way or ruffle any feathers. Definitely don't sing either - even if it's pretend singing. I am one of those people who loves to mouth the words of the songs I'm listening to while walking down the street, on the train, at the gym - wherever. Whenever I did this in London, I was greeted with glances that ranged from confusion to fear and even anger, as if I were some crazed sorceress. For something as simple as pretend singing? Yes people, yes. Do we realise how silly this sounds? There wasn't any sound being emitted, I wasn't creating any noise pollution. I wasn't hurting anybody. I wasn't stealing candy from children. I was just mouthing the words of my favourite songs under my breath. When did enjoying your own company in public get banned? When did we stop singing? Birds sing their hearts out, and no one could tell them otherwise. They just are. Why couldn't I be more like the birds? Stifling my voice this way is exemplary of adhering to tacit societal norms that encourage distancing ourselves from our inner children. I stopped singing even though doing so puts me in touch with my younger, more playful and giggly self. Singing can help you get through harsh times, it offers assistance for getting into the mood for whatever activity you are engaged in and it enables pent-up feelings to wistfully escape. When we see people thoroughly enjoying themselves without assistance from others, we may even deem them to be drunk. Maybe they *are* drunk - on Britney's 2007 album *Blackout*. While I was on my trip, I said to heck with it all. I felt inhibited and liberated. I didn't mind what anyone thought about my love of Britney or whoever else for that matter. This was one of the many malaises I had racked up in London for which travel was an elixir. Many times I went to the beach on my own and I wasn't bothered by who caught me listening to my iPod (yes, I still have one of those) and mouthing the lyrics of songs, swaying and singing (silently) to myself. In London, I would have been too hyper-aware for a faux solo sing-along. Now I thought, "What's the worst that could happen?" I realised that the people who would judge me off the bat for my gregariousness probably weren't the right people for me to surround myself with anyway. It felt great to let go of the fear of appearing to be off my rocker. I also developed an insatiable appetite for karaoke while I was away. It was the ultimate sign of how free I felt. Karaoke was something I seldom did in London but in Costa Rica, I couldn't get enough of it. My vocal cords were getting a lot of exercise; songs were performed in other languages I didn't even speak. It was a hoot. I also went to comedy clubs by myself and sat smack in the front without a single care about being heckled for coming alone. The purpose of this little anecdote is that we tend to have a lot more fun when we stop over-thinking and over-regulating our behaviour to adhere to "the rules". These days, I sing every day and everywhere and my singing isn't solely confined to the shower either.

Going on the trip enabled so much self-reflection which for me was previously unfeasible in London with the blaring cacophony clouding my judgement, it was my metanoia. I started to look at the world and myself with refreshed eyes and was able to identify the things that actually make me feel rife with aliveness: exotic music, multiculturalism, putting my language skills to use, palm trees, roaming, reinvention and the realisation of my dreams. This is not to say that these things are impossible to come by in London or any big city for that matter, but I was stuck in the daily grind and weighed down by the cog I was running in - London's also somewhat lacking in the palm tree department. I feel my best when days include inquisitiveness, curiosity, adventurousness, spontaneity, community and freedom; these are the things I value. In London, I was despondent because life lacked these vital elements. I felt trapped. Simply put, I was in the wrong place. It's important to do what feels right for *you*. Travelling heightens your sense of freedom because it opens you up to possibilities. My quest gave me a serious case of eleutheromania. Now that I was able to put my finger on the agitation I felt in London, I would design my life according to my values.

My extended stay in the Americas made it glaringly clear that by the water is where I thrive best. Proximity to the ocean, the mindset and the attire it requests has such a rejuvenating effect on me. I don't actually need to go into the water. I just like to know it's close by, perhaps as a sort of comfort blanket. I would go as far as to say that it's my happy place. I was much better suited to living in the Latin American tropics where each corner was flooded with lively music. *The* happy place will, of course, differ from person to person; it's anywhere you gain that feeling of tranquillity, comfort and inspiration. Going away massages the senses and helps to solve creativity issues. With the time I gained through shunning unnecessary busyness I started taking note of my daily activities, the places that stood out and the people I crossed paths with. The humble beginnings of that travel diary are the book you are reading today. Travelling encourages slight alterations in your thought processes that can, in turn, impact your reality. I recall once looking out a plane window; there were tiny little icicles on the window which I superimposed onto the body of water we were flying over. They ended up looking like hundreds of tiny little boats, converged for a seaside soirée. My imagination became the reality. They were no longer icicles, but something entirely more magical.

Travel makes us well versed in the world and in ourselves. We are introduced to people's complexities, especially our own. It opens the body and soul and heightens our cultural understanding. First-hand experience deepens our comprehension of what it is to be human. We see, hear, taste and experience the craziest things. Being on a trip is like a second lease at childhood; we're learning things, seeing things for the first time, playing more than we normally allow ourselves to and we'll have people convincing us to try weird foods. Our ears perceive new oddities because we also listen out more. We allow our senses to soak up our environment. Things we would never look twice at back home now glisten and twinkle. One such humdinger of a conversation I overheard involved two men discussing The Rolling Stones at a café. "Mick Jagger has a lot of girlfriends, most of them are just for one night", one said. Excuse me kind sir; a lady you know for one evening does not constitute a girlfriend, not even by a long shot. People also tell you the craziest stories. It was in San Juan del Sur, Nicaragua, where I first met a fecalfeliac - a person that's infatuated with human excrement. This particular girl was a fellow resident at the hostel I was staying at. Every encounter I had with her included some mention of faeces. She grasped every opportunity to dish about the brown stuff. This culminated with the afternoon she invited me to come and inspect her latest dumping. Apparently she'd had dragon fruit with breakfast and it turned that which is normally brown, to a shade of pink. With a rosy disposition she said, "I've saved it for you, would you like to come and see?" I couldn't make this stuff up.

My trip taught me to appreciate the beauty of small moments. No one can take those delightful (and often puzzling) days away from me. Our travels stay with us wherever we are and become part of our being. They serve to provide sweet memories when the chips are down too. Doing things I never thought I'd do in places I never thought I'd do them helped rebuild my confidence. Travel challenges you and particularly if you go on your own, you'll be faced with yourself. You'll grow, get a fresh start and make lifelong connections. Most of the other voyagers I met on my trip were going solo too. Travelling exposed me to people who had also ventured out to deal with their struggles and to be alone with their thoughts. It made me realise that these feelings of inadequacy are something everyone has at one point in their lives. I felt more connected to people. It wasn't me versus them, it was us versus life. If we accept that failure and pain are inevitable facts of all human life, we feel more connected to others as we then understand that everyone is struggling. Being apart from my friends and loved ones in London for so long also effortlessly singled out the people I actually missed in that time; the people I couldn't wait to put my arms around once more. Travel makes us reassess facts about our lives back home and calls our identity into question, our consumption identity too. Travel makes us aware of our excess baggage and the true weight it has on us. By the end of my trip, I was unfettered by regret about what happened with Carl because I was so grateful for all I had experienced and learnt. Upon my return, I chattered with frightening speed about all the things that excited me and which I couldn't wait to do again. Travel, in short, is educational. In fact, many choose to travel the world instead of going to university, feeling that it feeds them more. All in all, why did I need to wander to the other side of the world in order to confront these home truths? Because I was no longer operating on autopilot. Leaving our home comforts, readjusting our settings and switching up our routines so drastically forces us to engage with our decisions and our activities because we're actually thinking about them as opposed to being fuelled by muscle memory and the familiar. Some people might not be ready for the gravity of these realisations and may, therefore, shun these expeditions altogether.

Positive outcomes

After my mum passed away, I knew it was time. Time to go. Her parting advice had been to follow my heart and Panama was where it was. I was going to move there for real. An extended chain of events had taken place to get me there too. I discovered it after the upheaval of my break-up from Carl, just as I had rediscovered my love of writing through my fashion brand. I was going to move to Panama and become a writer. It made perfect sense. Losing mum was the push I needed to finally take the plunge and the reminder of life's fragility. My purpose was to enjoy my life every day and live according to my values; this plan suited me to a tee. Some very solemn months followed my mother's passing and then it was time to say goodbye to the life I had known for so long, sayonara London.

Picking up and leaving was the radical self-care I needed to nourish myself back to emotional health. I couldn't live in our house, walk down our street and be regularly confronted with the reminders of our shared life. The memories were all too charged. In Panama, I felt like I was living life right. I thrived there because I was doing what I was truly meant to be doing, in terms of what feeds my soul. I'd been restless in London for many years and was in a vicious circle of repetitive, uninspiring experiences until I was finally able to get off the Ferris wheel. I chose Panama whereas London was thrust upon me. Every day wasn't a cakewalk, but I was content because it was exactly where my soul craved to be. Because I had decided it myself, life was good and I was doing what I really was supposed to be doing (no inverted commas). This is my enduring love letter to Panama. My topophilia was intact, I was still completely enamoured of this place. I paid a visit to Bocas del Toro and I'd estimate that at least 50 per cent of the travellers I met back then still resided on those magical islands. They were now truly immovable, trapped and unable to enjoy any other earthly destinations. Travel may not be the solution to your problems; it just so happens that living in the wrong place was part of *my* problem. Travel does not mean running away from your dilemmas, it is, in fact, a competent means of confronting them head on.

Travelling to different places is like tasting lots of different teas to discover our preferred blend or going to a gallery and looking at the whole collection of paintings.

We don't just look at one; we observe the lot of them and only then do we know which one we like best. There might be hundreds of paintings hanging in that gallery, many of which we pass by without as much as a second glance. They don't strike us or speak to us at all, but when we find *our* painting, we inspect every stroke, studying the details with admiration. We gaze at it curiously and lovingly. That's what travelling is like. We walk and walk and hope to stop someplace where it feels right. Somewhere we feel compelled to stop. It isn't really a choice; it's out of our hands. Now that I have left my "supposed to" life in London behind, my days are mine to spend as I please, pursuing interests and hobbies of my own making. I am self-employed and choose the tropics as my office. My choice could be perceived as a somewhat dangerous one; I don't have the "security" of a pension and I'm moving to a country that speaks a language I am only partially fluent in (Reggaeton music, unfortunately, doesn't count) but *not* doing this would be the riskiest choice of all. According to my definition, I am now at my most successful, and the only success is the one *you* define.

The benefits of solo travel
Spending time alone is a form of self-care to improve the most important relationship in your life: the one you have with yourself. Prior to this trip, I had never really spent much time alone. During the journey, there were some days where I pretty much spoke to nobody but myself. I was the youngest of four children so growing up, our house was always buzzing with some sort of sound - be it from video games, laughter, TV, pots banging against

each other when mum cooked, or what have you. I was so used to being around people. Travelling alone taught me how to nurture my personal relationship, how to be my own friend. I learnt that I am capable of entertaining myself when it's just little old me. I allow the gift of beautiful music to be my companion and have a playlist to accompany any given mood. When I was a wee bairn, my sister and I would don our mum's heels and grown-up lady clothes, imagining we were older. We'd dance in front of the mirror putting on our own catwalk show while singing along to anything by Britney (oops, I mentioned her again). This cheerful habit has stayed with me till today. It brightens even the darkest of days. Travel helped me when the black dog was barking in my direction. Going away alone ironically alleviated my loneliness by reminding me that I will always have myself. I can have a good time wherever I go, whether I wear my solo jacket or big group party hat. I can survive with just myself to rely on, and there is great comfort in knowing that.

One may think of spending time alone as boring but *this* is the time for those great books. *This* is the time for stolen moments with golden music. *This* is the time for sunset gazing. *This* is the time for a self-odyssey. You *can* share moments with yourself. When was the last time you took a walk for fun? Or just closed your eyes and listened to the sound of your breath? Without distraction from others, you observe more. When we're on our own is when we engage in our best self-reflective practices: writing in a diary, listing, meditation. I am not advocating detaching yourself from all your people and circumnavigating the globe solo indefinitely. This is by no means an endorsement of eternal solitude; happiness, when shared, is twice the fun. But, once you learn how to be happy on your own, it will be impossible to tolerate those who make you feel anything less. Being able to withstand just your own company means you won't be desperate for anybody else's. When you're happy on your own, you'll wait for the *right* people and be selective with who you let infringe on your precious alone time. Through this one-woman adventure, I would gain mastery over myself and I'm felicitous to have come upon the realisation that we're never really alone because we have ourselves.

How to be a traveller

There are many ways to go about the migration of body and mind that is travelling. You don't actually have to go somewhere new to put yourself in the travel mindset. If you can't go abroad, you can be a tourist in your own town or city. Find a corner previously uncovered and explore it. For me, I ached to go to a different climate; years of evidence and a mean case of Seasonal Affect Disorder showed me that (trust me it's a real thing). I need a city in which I can see the water, one where warm air blows optimism my way. What do *you* need? What do you stand to gain from uprooting yourself onto unfamiliar territory? Picture a place in your mind's eye that you have always longed to venture to. What are the smells around you? Are there few detectable sounds, or is it buzzing with melodic aliveness? The breeze that hits your cheek, how warm or cold is it? Spin a globe and stop it with one finger. Look at where your finger lands, could you get yourself there? It worked for Prince Akeem in *Coming to America*; it could work for you too.

Travel gives you so much and requires a lot less of you than you think. It does take courage but it doesn't mean that you won't see your friends or family for months on end; Skype does exist after all. It doesn't have to require your entire bank account either. Travelling and having a career needn't be mutually exclusive, especially in today's age of the digital nomad and *The 4-Hour Workweek*-toting masses. You can always make more money, but you can't always make memories. Investing in exploration is priceless. "I really regret buying that plane ticket to a paradise island in the Caribbean", said nobody ever, literally. Nothing can substitute experience. Travel to make something happen when nothing does, travel when good things happen and also when bad things transpire. Travelling afar may not be the answer for *you*, so find your version of it; your tonic that opens you up to the beautiful, varied, rich, deep, fulfilling book that is the world.

CHAPTER SIX
THE THINGS THAT WE TELL OURSELVES ABOUT OUR LIVES

Here's a fact: many of the things you believe about yourself simply aren't true. These myths may have been cooked up by you or purported by others. In Chapter 1 we explored external validation and following imperatives set by others. Here, let's move slightly closer to home and examine the limitations we set for ourselves. To progress and live our best lives, it's important to be open to excavation and change; being able to purify the windows of consciousness, cleanse our minds, abandon our philosophies and discard our old stories.

What's your story?
My family moved to The Netherlands when I was quite young. It was a new, foreign land with harsh winters and harsh-sounding consonant sounds in its language. I couldn't help but notice how foreign I was too. I dressed differently, possessed a strange transatlantic accent and even styled my hair differently to everyone else in my class. Though I was enrolled in an international school where everybody was from everywhere, I felt I stood out like a sore thumb and hated the fact. Petrified of starting off on the wrong foot, I blended myself into the background as I navigated my way around this new environment. Amongst my group of friends, I was the most timid. I can hand on heart say that I didn't particularly like myself. I remember the day that all changed. I was 17 years old at a house party with my best friend (bomb scare Sarah) who was trilingual and terribly

witty. Two embarrassingly handsome boys were stood in front of us and I remember thinking about how nice it would be to be able to just talk to them - so I did. To my surprise, the conversation went smoothly; they didn't leave, scold me, or whatever nightmare scenario I thought would transpire when I opened up to people. At that moment, something struck me: things aren't so bad. I had friends, a loving and warm family, the opportunity to immerse myself in a melting pot of cultures, all my limbs, fingers and toes and I had a good head on my shoulders (if I may say so myself). Why had I been hiding behind a self-synthesised narrative of coming in last? I realised that I could change my life and the way I viewed myself. I did so that very evening, and the rest is history.

Back then I steadfastly compared myself to the girls around me in every aspect. During the teenage years, I poked holes in my appearance and never thought I was beautiful (skinny) enough. Thinking about it now, I was actually quite scrawny and wish I spent far more time lounging around in a two-piece than I did. The story I told myself was that I was never going to be "the beautiful one" and this was the narrative that guided my thoughts and actions. I told myself a lot of stories, bad ones at that. Drawing information from our past experiences as well as our immediate environment, we box ourselves into identities, story characters, so to say. If you've told yourself that you're always "the strong one", you may struggle to let yourself be taken care of. If you've always been the one who excelled at everything, failures might hit your self-esteem harder than the next person because you're so firmly tied to that notion of yourself as victorious. Ask yourself now, what stories have you told that may be keeping you stuck?

Another set of stories we tell involve our relationship with money and success. We tell ourselves that only when we attain/ buy/ win/ gain something else will we be happy. We strive and strive for monetary and professional success and never think about what happens once we get it. We imagine that our wholeness is inextricably linked to this eventual occurrence, forgetting that even the most "successful" people are just as capable of being unhappy. Wealth too has its burdens. Lottery winners gain cold hard cash but often lose friends, family, stability, safety and sanity, and we've all heard of the Oscar Love Curse, haven't we? Kate Winslet, Reese Witherspoon, Halle Berry, Susan Sarandon and Sandra Bullock are just a few women whose partners have divorced, cheated on or left them shortly after winning the Best Actress Academy Award, the pinnacle of a Hollywood actress's career. Many people are happy *despite* their success and not *because of* it.

We may also inherit stories; ideas that are passed down to us by existing comrades of a group we belong to regarding what it means to be a member of that said unit, leaving little perceived wiggle room for individuality. This includes prescriptions on what it means to be a member of our gender, religion, race or socio-economic group. In these cases, one may feel that they do not own their story, and they're simply out on the bench looking in wistfully along with all the other spectators. Sometimes, just because we are not like other people, it can make us think we are bad parents, children, employees or friends. Until we realise that we really don't "have to" be any certain type of way, this feeling of inadequacy will continue to plague us. Personally, there are a million things I'd rather do than cook. I noticed that whenever asked about the subject, I used to give a disclaimer that I do however like baking. This *is* true, I love to bake and adore the inviting aroma of a room where baked goods are being lovingly prepared, but why did I feel the need to highlight this when no one asked specifically if I liked to bake? This might have something to do with those two X chromosomes I've been carrying around. I was somehow lacking because as a woman, I was "supposed to" have been born with some home-making gene. I was pointing out my baking skills almost as if to say, "Though I may not be the perfect domestic goddess, I'm still salvageable cause I make a mean double chocolate gateau". Because I don't adhere to this gender-centric stereotype, I'd augment the story to circumnavigate the truth and make myself feel better. At least I'd be able to feed my husband with *something* when he came back from a hard day wrestling bears to ensure we were well fed.

Gender conditioning plagues men and women alike. The inscriptions of macho culture mean that the sexuality of a man is called into question if he enjoys a manicure a little bit *too* much, hasn't played the field sufficiently and isn't preoccupying himself with running the risk of impregnating some woman somewhere. Countless men I know never grant themselves the freedom to cry simply because they're not "supposed to". That's their story and their sticking to it. Interestingly, stereotypes themselves often have their origins in myths and fairytales. Similarly, not everything we think about ourselves is accurate. Some of our "truths" turn out to be make-believe hoaxes. It is wise to question why these stories benefitted us in the first place.

Why we tell the tales we tell

We concoct stories, lies or half-truths about ourselves because we're uncomfortable with the present reality of our lives. Am I rich, beautiful, successful, intelligent, charming, unforgettable enough? We tell social lies because we feel inadequate about something *today*. It's too risky to show our real self because it's not as glitzy as we'd like it to be. Even embellishments are a form of being economical with the truth. "Where do you work?" "Oh I'm an architect but I'm working at this restaurant around the corner just a couple of days a week cause it's really close by and it's a fun place to work between gigs". You're fluffing the answer with filler details because you're judging the situation. *You* don't think it's OK to be a server. You might be lying to others or to yourself. Either way, cosying up with rationalisation and denial is much more comfortable than facing a reality you perceive to be unbearable, so you'll spearhead your own PR campaign and control the way you would like to be perceived - even by yourself.

Another reason we fabricate truths is to arm ourselves with valid excuses that prevent us from going forth with plans that scare and intimidate us. Self-handicapping protects us from truly discovering our limitations because we never make the attempts needed to do so. We tell ourselves that something needs to happen before we can be happy at some future date because it absolves us from blame if we do not feel happy right now. We tell damning tales about our capabilities that cause over-familiarity with phrases such as "I cannot", "I will never be able to", "maybe one day", and "I'm too old for that". Self-imposed limitations based on age certainly fall into this category. How old we are becomes a crutch because society says we can't do that anymore: women wearing mini skirts after a certain age, men using scooters after a certain age, backpacking after a certain age. We've got to sow our wild oats while we're young and then live a quiet life when we're older. At some point, it's time to "settle down", whatever that means. If you had a penny for every time you've heard someone say, "if I was younger I would do blah blah blah", how much money would you have today? Have you said it yourself? Do you realise you're denying yourself freedoms simply because of the year you were born, something you had no control over? People often perceive there to be an expiry date on certain behaviours or things that aren't acceptable for them based on who they are and what life stage they're at. Before I moved to Panama many told me they wished that they too could live abroad some time. Well, why can't they? Nothing makes me special. They can do it if they *really* wish to. The very essence of life stems from the mind's energy. Thoughts are vibrations that mobilise things and send invitations out to the universe. Adopting limiting thoughts and beliefs means cloaking all outcomes in negativity, affixing a flat tire onto your car, so you can drive it fast to nowhere. I encourage you to pay attention to the stories you choose to formulate about your life because the most powerful words are the ones you use to speak to yourself.

The stories we tell ourselves about our lives store a hotbed of information; they have the power to reveal a) what we fear the most and b) what we truly desire. That little fib about your less than ideal current employment situation may reveal a fear of separation and rejection (a) and a belief that you deserve more than you currently have (b). If you've always told yourself that you're "the strong one" and that everything will collapse if *you* don't keep it together, you may be harbouring a fear of actually not being needed at all, feeling powerless (a) and seeking control to mitigate these feelings of helplessness (b). The story I told myself about being the shy gal masked a fear of rejection due to perceived differences (a) and a longing to feel truly among in my new foreign surroundings (b).

In order to truly move towards our ideal futures, we need to be honest with ourselves, omitting all rationalisations and buffering. The things is, all that time spent trying to manipulate opinion is removing our focus from our real business of enjoying *our lives*. How can we get to the root of the problems under the hood with a can of spray paint? Stories can keep us stuck but they needn't do so because they can be written, re-written and re-issued with new editions for years on end, over and over again. Patterns of thinking need not be permanent. Armed with this knowledge, we can choose to reclaim the ink and pen an improved story, then tell it loud and long enough that it seeps into our consciousness and the universe has no choice but to say yes to what we put out there.

Turning the page

We have a lot more choice than we realise in terms of
how to live well because there is more than just one way
to live. If you let it, the plot can thicken and your story
might get that bit juicier and fulfilling. Your hero may
take a different form and may not be a prince or princess
at all, but your own inner strength. This book is about
breaking free from prescribed modes of behaviour that
are inapplicable to us - societal prescriptions as well as
self-imposed ones. Today, I have a strong awareness of
the stories I told myself about my life and how they kept
me stuck. I was "supposed to" be successful which meant
getting a fancy schmancy corporate job and making
money. I told myself I was a failure because I didn't cut it
in that world. I told myself that rejection was a bad thing,
an assault on the ego and its penchant to be desired. I
told myself that love lost was the end of the world. I told
myself that I could never travel by myself; solo travel was
for chumps. I told myself I needed a reason, a job or a
person to move somewhere. These stories or limiting
perceptions clearly did me more harm than good. I shall
now reserve my pencils for creating positive blueprints,
and I am happy to make amendments along the way.

Stories can turn into habits, ones that we don't realise we
can change. The fact that our lives are shaped by
narratives means that our stories can be edited and
completely transformed, which can, in turn, change the
way we see our lives and the possibilities within them. As
earlier stated, progression requires an openness to change
and a willingness to waltz with the uncertain. Pursuing
what will set your soul alight demands a tolerance of new

characters, new elements and an all-new ending. Experimenting with new stories and identities is thoroughly possible and absolutely encouraged. You don't have to be exactly who you were last year or even the year before that. If you were captain of the football team, you can decide to pick up the clarinet and be all about that now. Nobody has fixed ability either. Anna Pavlova wasn't born performing the perfect pirouette all at once. Your abilities are as malleable as you are. Sticking to the story of who you once were or are "supposed to" be is tantamount to keeping yourself stuck; condemning yourself as a member of a group, which you may actually be overqualified to belong to.

History has blessed us with dazzling quotes on transformation and hope from poets, philosophers and artists. You can be that artist. If you are to be the great storyteller of your life, choose to compose a symphony of triumphs. The brilliance of the symphony stems from its varying constituents, the different instruments, the peaks, troughs and fluctuating sounds: essentially, the changes.

2

Part Two

Accept

CHAPTER SEVEN
THE THINGS THAT WE GAIN WHEN WE EMBRACE CHANGE

So you've realised some things. You've read through your pages and uncovered some naked truths. Some were positive, others may be less so. This section centres on accepting those shreds of wisdom and accepting yourself with all your quirks in order to be able to put your plans into motion. While change can be uncomfortable, it also pays large dividends. Things we gain by embracing change include growth, flexibility and adaptability as well as new opportunities. Change pushes us out of our comfort zones and makes us test our old theories.

Changes for the better
When we embrace change, we offer less resistance and thus our suffering is reduced when things don't go our way. There's a difference between being OK with things that have happened and truly accepting them. Resisting hurts more. Acceptance is not a given, it's a choice. We have a lot more fun when we don't fight the inevitable (easier said than done, I know). Embracing change involves relinquishing the need to control things. Part of accepting yourself and your life is getting a handle on the things you can and can't control. Some things are worth trying to manipulate and some things aren't. What you *can* control is the people you hang around with and the situations you put yourself in. What *can't* be controlled is what people think or feel about you (you're not a witch doctor). Acceptance isn't the same as resignation. You are not accepting stoic and mediocre, you are accepting

what is, that which you cannot change, your past for example.

We get to make peace with the past when we embrace change. When someone says something that strikes a nerve, it's often because it is triggering something uncomfortable from our days gone by. The most painful memories are the hardest to admit, but therefore also the most freeing once we accept and let them go. The deep pain of these memories explains why they hold us in their clutches. What happened in the past is *part* of who you are, but not *the sum* of who you are. In fact, you are changing right now. Rejecting change is also essentially holding on to the past and bypassing the present, this very moment. There is a new day knocking on your door for you to let in.

There have been many changes that took place in my life which were unplanned and initially unwanted, but have lead me to where I am now (which FYI is a much better place). For one, my job in advertising going down the drain lead me to further my education which in turn opened the door to an illustrious career as a fashion designer. Now I am the proud wearer of many professional hats. I thought I would be a high-flying advertising executive right now. These days, I'm a writer and I wake up in the morning whenever I wish to. I am my own boss, and I write about the very deepest passions of my soul. My dad was posted around a lot for his job and when I was about 11 years old, he had the option to choose where he went next. My siblings and I obviously hoped he'd be sent to the States. Truth be told, I wanted to be a real cheerleader. I wanted to recreate the things I saw on TV, go to parties with red solo cups and be all about that life. Our American dream was not to be alas and we were sent to The Netherlands instead. While there I learnt to speak Dutch, travelled all around Europe and got to exercise my passion for languages. Things simply don't always go according to plan and that's fine. Derailed plans often lead to the most beautiful of occurrences so do leave room in your sketches for drawing outside the lines.

The unpredictability of life is what makes it so zesty and scrumptious. Change keeps things exhilarating and interesting. It's OK if you don't know exactly what you'll be doing in five years. You don't have to have all the answers right now. Things would probably be a tad boring if you did. People adore the changing of the seasons because each one is a new beginning, a chance to shed our old skin and begin anew. It's fresh air to fuel fresh thinking. Change gives us much to look forward to; it's an opportunity for rebirth. Switching up our routines, adding something new to our repertoire and alternating our paths can empower us. Change wakes us up from functioning on autopilot. The reason we may stay within the confines of safe routines is because change terrifies us. After all, things could go wrong. We could get disappointed. We might prefer things how they used to be. Change can be overwhelming but welcoming it can expose us to extraordinary experiences that are outside of our conventional worldview. Newer, more beautiful existences are ours for the taking if only we learn to love change.

We adapt better to the changes we plan ourselves, it's the unwanted changes that are hard to deal with. Carl's departure was one such change. It was a decision that was forced upon me and I was blindsided by it. This one small occurrence was actually a grand seismic shift in my world. I resisted the change because I never signed up for it. Majority of my anguish was caused by holding on to the idea of us and what we had once been. I prioritised a romanticism of the past over respecting his wishes to be separate from me and also dishonoured my own right to be happy separate from him. Some changes are harder to accept than others. My mother's cancer diagnosis was one such maladjustment. In the short term, all else was put on hold as we prioritised her care and making the most of our final days together. In the long run, I would need to accept the loss of the life I had envisaged for myself. A life in which she was ever-present, quoting Macbeth for the umpteenth time and telling us the same old stories over and over. Losing my mother was a tough tribulation. Life wasn't over, but it was different. In many ways, it forcibly accelerated my maturity because change helps you learn. There is no growth without change.

Getting unstuck

Often, growth and comfort do not co-exist. Accept that in order to get what you desire, you might be uncomfortable for a while. There may be a necessity to move. There might be marking time. The greater the importance an action has on the development of our soul, the scarier it is. As frightening as it might be to quit your job, move, let go of someone or be your true Unconditioned Self, the result of not doing so is even more unsettling in the long run. We often know what would make us happier and how to make the changes but simply don't take the steps required out of fear.

Any type of change (whether bad or good) will arouse some complicated feelings, no matter how thrilling it is on the surface. Despite my sheer excitement, moving to Panama was not without headaches. It took quite a while to adjust to regular power outages after years of living in Europe. One evening the electricity went off while I was taking a shower at a friend's place. I had to make my way out of the bathroom without any lights to guide me and ended up stepping on her cat. Kitty didn't like that one bit and let out the most terrorising squeal. We laugh about this story now, but at the time we were petrified. In London, I had become accustomed to actual pavements without holes in them. In Panama City, you could be walking down a beautiful, sun-bathed street and then find that you've stepped into a rancid pothole; shoes ruined, leg toxic and dignity annihilated. Change can be distressing; one minute you might be laughing and then crying the next. Cry your heart out if you must, but accept what is happening to you. Defiance is pointless. Instead of resisting change, find the lesson you needed to learn from it. If you can identify a positive benefit for something that's ending, you're much more likely to receive your new situation with open arms. Believe that the universe has its reasons for putting you where you were. Regarding relationships, remember the old adage that people come into your life for a season, a reason or a lifetime. With acceptance comes calmness. Change is necessary to keep you alive and flourishing. Accepting change means moving towards it and not running from it; embracing it wholeheartedly, with all blemishes evident.

To take stock of your relationship with change, ask yourself the following questions:

1. Are you change-averse?
2. What do you need to change in order to live the life you desire?
3. What changes might you be resisting right now?
4. What has change taught you?
5. What positive outcomes have you experienced as a result of a plan being derailed?
6. What do you stand to gain by becoming more open to change?

Acceptance is essentially giving consent for what will be to be. Change is life's certain promise. Everything is always in flux. The unpredictability of life is part and parcel of its beauty. Nothing is ever perfect and it doesn't need to be either.

CHAPTER EIGHT
THE THINGS THAT WE GAIN WHEN WE ACCEPT OURSELVES

The world is full of people who are uncomfortable in their own skin. Accepting ourselves means giving up on being perfect and just letting ourselves be. We don't need to gain, succeed or acquire to accept ourselves. We can also lose, cry and thirst and still accept ourselves all the same. Acceptance is unconditional. True acceptance is knowing all about yourself and loving yourself in spite of *and* because of all of that. Accepting yourself requires knowing who yourself is. Have you answered the questions posed in the preceding chapters? What have you learnt about yourself (if anything)? Accepting ourselves is simply not judging the way we are. My friend Annie brought to my attention the fact that I say sorry a lot. When I accidentally brush up against someone, when somebody tells me they have a headache, when I tell a story that takes too long, I tend to apologise. On the flip side, I also say thank you a lot too. Apparently, I'm too nice. True as that may be, I can't be anyone else but me. Trying to change this aspect of myself would be contrary to my values. I can still get ahead without compromising my niceness. Meekness is not weakness and I shall continue to be sweet as pie within limits (I won't be taken advantage of).

Accepting yourself means standing your ground and not stepping outside the lines of your morals for any reasons other than your own comfort. If you accept an invitation to do something beyond the line of your values, you are putting *yourself* in an uncomfortable position. If your presence is requested at a post-work jaunt to a strip club and you go just because everybody else is, or you think it will get you in the good books with your boss or your clients, chances are you'll stand out like a sore thumb. You'll spend the majority of the evening feeling awkward which will be visible for all to see anyway. The jig will be up. The same applies to taking drugs if that's not your cup of tea. This is not to say that new experiences are to be shunned, but there are certain telltale signs to spot when you are caving into peer pressure or just going along with the crowd. Would you still do it if you knew people could find out? What is your gut telling you? Are you embarrassed or ashamed of it? Deep down you know the things you think are right and wrong for you, the rules of your club. Accepting ourselves is not changing who and how we are because society says so. Accepting ourselves means being honest. Acceptance is peacefully admitting that you are you.

One of the things you gain through self-acceptance is a better relationship with yourself and with others. A merry and loving heart is the greatest gift you can bestow upon anyone. That anyone can be you. The condition of the relationship you have with yourself governs all other relationships in your life. For instance, the way you relate to yourself influences your physical health, the food you put into your body, how often you exercise, how you spend your money and how much time you expend on yourself. Your ability to love and accept yourself also impacts how much you let others love you. You aren't intimidated by excess love because you believe you deserve it. Life gets better because you love yourself unconditionally. Acceptance is trusting yourself. Self-doubt will contaminate and erode your relationships. We waste so much time in our lives questioning things, time that we could spend enjoying our days and enjoying each other's company. Accepting ourselves also means accepting others for who they are. Not everyone can be like you and they don't have to respond to things the way you do either. Be generous enough to know that people are trying their best. Love is a waltz with joy, a dance that encourages empathy for others and intimacy with yourself. Self-acceptance means building yourself strong, and the stronger you build yourself from within, the lesser the likelihood of drowning in a sea of external pressures. Happiness is an inside job; it's a wholly internal process. You won't be happy just because someone buys you flowers or pays you a compliment. These things are fleeting and are more about *feeling* happy than *being* happy, and there is a world of difference between the two. Being happy and satisfied comes from abandoning unworthiness and self-criticism. Embracing the way you are wired, your curiosities and passions leads to a much more fulfilling existence.

Accepting one part of yourself means accepting it all, the whole shebang. This includes your emotions. To allow yourself to feel is to allow yourself to be alive. Pain doesn't go away just because you don't acknowledge it. Denying your emotions doesn't make them any less real. Renouncing our truths causes discomfort for us as well as the people around us. Our general wellbeing suffers and so does our physical health. For months my body was telling me I couldn't cope with the stress and fever pitch intensity of The Agency until my system could take no more. Only when I developed chest palpitations as a result of the anxiety did I listen. Numbing yourself is also a form of running away from your problems and thus opting for comfort over courage. You're no closer to getting over a feeling if you're beating yourself up for feeling that way in the first place. Accepting yourself is also about not judging your feelings, but accepting them for what they are. Don't address your emotions with over-amplified disappointment or self-pity. Don't blame yourself if you feel low. Recognise it, feel it and let the moment pass. Rejecting the feeling isn't dealing with it either. Let yourself go through the motions. It's tempting to shy away from our feelings; confronting them directly can leave our vulnerabilities exposed, but repressing them is futile.

Unconditional (self) love

"Our lack of self-love - our disconnection from love - is the core of almost all our problems. It is the root of all our neurosis. It is the root of our relationship problems. It is the root of settling for a life of bread and cheese rather than inviting ourselves to the banquet. It leads to mundane lives of quiet desperation". These firm remarks are courtesy of Gill Edward's book *Wild Love* (2006, p. 168). She expands noting that we limit ourselves to what others will "allow" us and detain ourselves in lacklustre routines and stultifying relationships when we do not love ourselves. These sentiments are mirrored in *Loveability* by Robert Holden (2013, p. 49) who describes self-love as a "loving attitude from which positive actions arise that benefit you and others". Holden, a specialist in the field of positive psychology, maintains that the Unconditioned Self is different from our imagined self. The Unconditioned Self is our eternal loveliness and it loves us unconditionally. It does not try to win love from others either because we *are* love. We can't settle for less than we deserve when we love ourselves unconditionally.

Underpinning many people's feelings of not being loveable is the absence of self-compassion. Part of accepting ourselves is forgiving our mistakes. So you made an error of judgement or you took a wrong step somewhere; you *had to* try it out in order to know it wasn't for you. Everything you have realised about your failures, your rejections and losses, your relationships, all the untruths you have told: forgive yourself for all those things, for you had to experience them to know. Forgive yourself for whatever you think you have done wrong or more importantly - what your self-image thinks you've done wrong. Opting to forgive is choosing love over pain, love over guilt, love over fear. A magical way to silence the voices of self-doubt in your head is by showing yourself kindness when you perceive you are falling short (perceive being the operative word). The voices in your head might be going into overdrive criticising you, telling you that you're not good enough, that you can't do it or that you'll never get there. Kindness counteracts all this. Speak to yourself as gently as you would to a small child, offer words of encouragement and compassion. When things go wrong, be even kinder to yourself. This fortifies your ability to deal with those tough situations. We tend to show our friends and family a greater level of care than we give ourselves. We speak to ourselves in a blameful, hostile tone that we would never dream of using with others (at least to their faces). Self-acceptance is a celebration of your flaws and your fortitude. It is not about thinking you are better than anyone else, but rather listening to your heart's intellect which tells you that you're lovable no matter what.

Self-love is not to be confused with arrogance or false pride. It's OK to love yourself. It's actively encouraged, in fact. Can you look yourself in the eye and say, "I love myself" without feeling uncomfortable? People who boldly declare their love for themselves are deemed to be full of conceit or narcissists. There is, however, a clear difference between the two. Narcissism is a neurosis; it looks like self-love but feels emptier as it's a front for a deeper fear of being unlovable (Holden, 2013). Don't be afraid of self-love; it's how you're *meant* to feel about yourself. Self-love in Spanish is *auto-amor*, signalling that loving yourself is an automatic attitude. It is instinctive and not at all shameful. Babies wear no masks. They are totally naked and free of armour. They aren't trying to put on a face, pretending to be anything other than themselves. Babies demonstrate the simple fact that being lovable is our basic nature. It is when they get older and are conditioned by the world around them that they start to identify with the learned self and view being lovable as something that is conditional. Remember this when next you think about self-love and arrogance in the same sentence. You are the one consistent person in your entire life. Therefore, loving yourself isn't vain; it's sane.

Know that you deserve your love and affection just as much as anyone else does. Tattoo it in your mind, on your wall or on your fridge. Plaster it wherever you can in order to remind yourself that you are worth love and happiness. It matters more that you accept yourself than if others accept you. Your relationship with yourself is the most important one you'll ever have.

Self-love does not require any conditions. It's not an effect of anything; it is self-determined. Accept your body, it's your home. Where would you be without it? Accept your mind; it's the genius behind your wit and wisdom. Accept your heart and listen to it more often. Fill up your tank with love, self-love that is (cheesy I know, but resoundingly apt). Accept and acknowledge that your life is valuable. Self-love isn't about just giving yourself gifts and pleasures. Holidays, delicious food, even massages are not the spoils of self-love. *Auto-amor* is at the core of who you are. When we love ourselves, we accept ourselves too. Self-acceptance is embracing ourselves unconditionally in all circumstances, not just when things go right and we excel. Self-acceptance differs from self-esteem, which is more tied up with how we judge ourselves within a given area of our lives. This in itself means that our self-perception is highly unsteady because it is based on succeeding or failing at something and thus, it is relative to other people. This also means we may situate ourselves as inferior or superior to others. Self-acceptance is having an acute awareness of the fact that you might not be the fastest, funniest or most financially buoyant etc, but being at peace with that. These words are worth reading several times over. To assist with your journey of self-acceptance, ask yourself the following questions: is your relationship with self-love linked to how others view you? Are there any elements of yourself you are yet to make peace with? Do you truly accept yourself?

<u>Surplus gains</u>
When you accept yourself it frees up all this space to just be you. You're an irreplaceable original, there's nobody out there that's exactly like you (even if you have a twin). A cover song might be better than the original, but it'll never be the same arrangement. There will always only ever be one of that precise song in the world. When your family or teachers told you that you were special as a child, they weren't lying. It is a privilege and a pleasure to discover your special light and mark on the world. You have the right to be who you are. Accept that you are different from other people and as such you have your own standards to live by, not theirs. Everything about you is unique: your smile, your heart, your quirks, your intricacies and your vision. Being who you are is the privilege of a lifetime. Loving yourself is believing that it is an honour to know and be you. I can say, "It is an honour to know me" without the slightest discomfort. It is not conceited nor is it bigheaded. It's a fact because I am a presence of love for others and myself. Your life on earth is about you; you are the one who struggles through your pain and dazzles with delight when times are good. Accepting yourself means quitting with those damning self-judgements. Accepting yourself means walking into a room full of people and thinking "I hope I like them and I have fun" rather than "I hope they like me". Your

wishes are as valid as anyone else's. Your life is yours to live. As long as you don't hurt anyone, what's the harm in being unapologetically you? I accept that living a carefree life under the palm trees is where I see myself. I accept that the 9-5 is not for me. I accept that I may never become a millionaire. I accept that I will continue to make mistakes. I accept it all. Self-love is a commitment to show up for yourself, to give yourself all you ever dreamed of because you deserve it. Because you love yourself, you promise to lavish yourself with the gifts of kindness and compassion, just as you would to others. You don't have to be the most attractive, smartest or the richest, but if you truly love and accept yourself, you'll feel like the richest and most importantly, you'll be free.

3

Part Three

Pursue

CHAPTER NINE
THE THINGS THAT SET US FREE

Free to live your best life, that is. Now we're moving on into phase three, the final leg of our journey. We've delved into the various corners of our lives, uncovered some basic truths, taken steps to accept them and now here's what to do about them. This is undoubtedly the section to bookmark. This is about following through with your liberation and the little and big things you can do to feel better in *your* life every day - that's why you're reading this book after all. Here I offer 13 steps to take towards living according to your truth. You are more than welcome to use none or all of them as you navigate your way towards the life you'd like to live.

1. Engaging in self-reflection

The first step towards getting what you desire is knowing what you desire. Humans are atrocious at knowing what will actually make them happier - that's where self-reflection has relevance. In *The Happiness Myth*, there is a line that stresses the importance of self-reflective practices charismatically: "Know yourself. This is the key to all philosophy, the centre of all wisdom, the one thing that decides if you are the actor in a tragedy or a comedy" (Hecht, 2008, p. 21). I do not consider this to be an overstatement and myself propose self-reflection as one of the most important aspects of the entire journey of free will. This is because clarity is what unfastens us from bondage. Engaging in self-reflection involves asking yourself questions continuously because you are ever changing. Remember that knowing yourself better means knowing others better too. You can also better place yourself within situations that are commensurate with your ideals, desires, hopes, likes and loathes. A little bit of self-reflection goes a very long way.

My friends Laura, Sonia and Jenny tease me mercilessly about my love of list making, but lists are not to be scoffed at, oh no. Besides being a calming pastime, they help you tabulate your plans and visually depict what you need to do get *there* (wherever it is *you* desire to go). They are also a great way to jog your memory. At the end of each year, I make a list of everything I have accomplished in those 12 months and this puts me in a capable mindset for the following 365 days. I also make a list of my happiest memories for that year which just puts me in a good mood, and why not? You can create any kind of list that positively reflects the things you value (friendship, warm memories, successes etc) and injects hopeful optimism into your days.

I'm a big fan of listing in general, but to-do lists sit right at the top of my naughty list (I don't actually have a naughty list, don't worry). To-do lists can be great, but they can also end up stressing you out if things aren't getting ticked off. I prefer to write a list of things I like to do, so every time I feel down I can go on out and do them. I suggest you make lists that you will actually enjoy ticking things off of and ones you'll enjoy looking back at. Every day, add something to a growing list of things you like about yourself for example. Knowing what you are good at is an art form in itself. There is nothing wrong with taking a moment to appreciate all the great things about yourself. Make a list of your strengths but make a list of your weaknesses too, as this is part of self-acceptance. Are you bad at receiving criticism, constructive or otherwise? Do you struggle to say no to people? There are so many types of lists which act as exercises for delving deeper into yourself. Below, I offer three sets of lists for you to engage with your past (commemorative lists), your present (personal lists) and think about your future (goal-oriented lists).

Commemorative lists
1. Things I have done that I am most proud of
2. What I accomplished last year
3. Happiest moments of the last year
4. Remarkable people I have met
5. Risks I have taken (that either paid off or didn't)
6. Some of my happiest memories
7. Best and worst decisions I have made
8. My success timeline
9. Best sunsets I have seen

Personal lists
1. My strengths and weaknesses
2. Things that make me happy
3. My hobbies and things I like to do
4. Quirky facts about me
5. Things I am grateful for
6. Songs that cheer me up
7. Traits I like my friends and partners to have (the rules of my relationship club)
8. Ways I like to relax when I feel stressed
9. Things I like about myself
10. What my definition of success is
11. What motivates me
12. How I congratulate myself when things go right

13. How I show appreciation

<u>Goal-oriented lists</u>
1. Places I would like to visit one day (bucket list)
2. New things I would like to try
3. Some of my fears and how I can overcome them
4. My priorities for life (this year and always)
5. Skills I would like to develop
6. Personal promises to keep
7. A letter to my future self outlining my hopes dreams imagining they came true
8. How I can inject more pleasure into my life so I enjoy it more
9. What are my goals?
10. What are my values?
11. What do I hope for and desire in life?

Add note making to your habits. Jot down new ideas as soon as they pop into your head. Keep a notebook beside your bed or in the bathroom for those moments of inspiration when you're brushing your teeth, or just before you go to bed. Keep a laughter diary of all the things that have made you laugh recently. Anything at all that put a smile on your face. Writing does help. Take some time to sit with your thoughts and ask yourself questions. Be nosey, you might be amazed by what you discover. Find out what makes you tick. I'm always astonished when I ask people the question "what do you like?" and they draw blanks. Generally get to know yourself better. To help get your creative juices flowing, here are some questions to spur on your own self-reflection session.

How do you **feel** right now? Label your emotions.

Sometimes you know you feel down but can't quite put your finger on what's wrong so it helps to retrace your steps. Why do you think you feel the way you do about certain things? How do your emotions affect your relationships and your behaviour? Your feelings aren't the enemy. Befriend them. Look inwardly at your emotions and what they tell you about yourself, use them to help you transform or create something in your life.

Regarding your **relationships,** do you like what you're doing right now and with whom? Do you have healthy relationships in your life? Do you have a network that can support you through whatever you decide to do? Do you play a role in front of different people? Which version do you feel is most true to you?

Regarding your **successes**, what are you most proud of creating? My greatest pride comes from rebuilding myself after my upheavals and creating beautiful relationships with the people in my close circle. What does success mean to you? What are you good at? What are your aspirations?

Regarding your **failures**, how have they held you back in the past? What have you learnt from them? Have this conversation with yourself, no matter how uncomfortable.

Regarding your **weaknesses**, what can you do to stop them getting in the way of you attaining what you desire? What are your fears? What are your triggers? Do you allow self-sabotage to thwart your missions? Think about what mistakes you have made so you can learn from them.

Regarding **work**, are you doing what you love? What do you love doing? Are you working with or against yourself? What do you like the least and most about your job?

Regarding your **hobbies**, what are they? What do you love doing just for the sake of doing it? Where do you spend your time?

Regarding **happiness**, what actually makes you happy versus what do you think "should" make you happy? What makes you feel the most alive? Are you happy right now?

Regarding your **purpose**, what is the meaning of life to you? What does living well mean to *you*? Who are you? What do *you* believe in? What inspires you? What is your truth?

Regarding your **life** in general, are you comfortable where you are? What elements do you need in order to feel more alive and excited about your life? Are you currently the best version of yourself?

One of the most observable criticisms of self-reflection is that it is an inward, self-gratifying egotistic pursuit which puts the needs of the individual above all else. Well, let me ask you this, would you get on a plane piloted by someone without a licence? Would you accept travel recommendations from a travel writer that had never left their hometown? Would you take mortgage advice from a vet? These people have become professionals in their field by working on their own project first and thus are better situated to help others. If you'd like to be someone that makes an impact in the lives of others, it serves you to put your own oxygen mask on first. You are no good to your best friend, your parents, your partner, your boss or your community when you are riddled with anxiety, self-doubt and loathing. There is nothing wrong with taking stock of who you are and where you are in life and most importantly - accepting your situation. The better you feel about your life, the more useful you will be to the people around you. I was of no use to my friends and my family when I was gloomy and sleep-deprived working at The Agency. Having now spent some time on my project, I have more space to invite more of the things and people I love into my life and be present with them. Working on your project contributes to the quality of your experience here and you are never too young or old for that. Imagine you are a seed. A seed knows what makes it strong; it knows to move towards the light, which feeds it. It also knows how to absorb even when it's dark. Getting to know yourself better is a means of nourishing that seed and gaining clarity into your personal situation.

The first part of my life was spent learning about the outside world; I wish to spend this part of my life learning about myself. I'd like to understand what makes *me* tick in this world and I'll be better for it. As I become a person that knows my own mind, I gain greater awareness of what my intentions are. Intentions are the gateway to the mind, what controls our perceptions. If you don't attend to something, you can't be aware of it. Attention is powerful: it controls your reality so attend to yourself. Take a journey within yourself to find out who you really are. You might not be destined to become anything new, but rather unbecome everything that you're not so that you can be who you were meant to be.

2. Embracing our fears

Once you've taken an introspective look at the general temperature of your crevices, you become alert to your dreads and fears. There are many basic fears humans share: the fear of being unloved, not being enough, loss, change and the fear of dying. The fear of these things is the fear of life itself because they are part and parcel of an individual's existence. There will always be someone who doesn't love you, sometimes you won't be enough, things will indeed leave your life and you will lose them if they are not meant for you, things will change and one day you will no longer be alive. Embrace your humanity by easing up to the eeriness of your fears.

The fear of failure is something many people wrestle with. As previously mentioned, it is actually a fear of shame that underpins the fear of failure. Shame, unworthiness and fear can, however, be unlearnt. It is our responsibility to reset the self-worth scale. One of the biggest factors behind success is believing. Have faith in yourself and others will too. Feed your faith and your fears will starve to death. Believe you deserve it, that you can do it and that you'll get there. If you don't even try, you've already failed. Don't fixate on all the reasons why it won't work and choose to rather focus on the one reason why it will. If you think you'll fail, chances are that you probably will. What you think is what you get. If you're going to doubt anything, then doubt your limits. Your accomplishments start when you decide to try. Fear is a liar telling you that you can't.

Being afraid is the easiest way to remain stuck. If your fear of crossing the road engulfs you and is greater than your desire to reach your destination, then you'll stay put where you are. You'll never move until you muster the strength to get yourself to where you hope to be. Find the courage; the courage required to embark on something new, the courage to do the things that frighten you, the courage to get up after you've been down. Let your choices be a reflection of your wishes and not your fears. When we allow fear to control us, we stay safe and comfortable, but facing fears opens the door to things that could be scary *and* amazing. Travelling across the world on my own was frightening but oh-so-rewarding in the long run. Go on and go places you never thought possible. Fear keeps folks doing things with people in places they would be better to have left years ago.

Think of all the things you gain when you face your fears. If you were scared of falling you probably wouldn't have learnt how to walk, so hold on to that fearlessness you had as a child. Babies are eager to take those steps and they get back up after each setback because they aren't afraid to fall or look stupid. Looking stupid takes a lot of courage. I am proud to say I have done many frightening things that I thought would make me look like an utter mooncalf. I took that chance, I quit my job, I booked that trip, I confessed my feelings, I walked away from people, I cried in public, I put my heart on the line and bags of self-awareness were gained by doing so. Don't worry about losing face. You are first young and stupid before you are old and wise. Strive to look stupid. I would rather have a life of "oh wells" than "what ifs".

Rather than letting them cripple you, walk *towards* your fears. It is precisely the things you fear that will challenge and enrich you. You fear them for a reason and thus they hold power over you. Once you face them, their voltage is diminished. The negative thought patterns we get stuck in stem from fear; this includes fear of what other people are thinking. Fear makes strangers out of people who would be great friends. Shyness is also connected to fear, but in time you might see that people aren't so scary. "Becoming friends with a dragon is smarter than killing it. Rather than fight your fears, ride them towards a better understanding of yourself" (Dimitri, 2015, p.15). Fear and regrets are inhibiting. In the end, it's the not the things we *did* that we regret, it's the things we *didn't* do. So, what are you afraid of?

3. Being honest with ourselves and others

Being the protagonist of your story is a matter of the heart *and* the mind. It is about being honest with yourself and accepting some potentially tricky facts about your life and choices. Truly, nothing good can come from deceiving yourself. Staying in a job I despised for as long as I did was lying to myself and telling myself things were OK because I was doing "the right thing". Denial is a survival mechanism for only so long. Telling the truth is unburdening. Be honest with yourself about your very nature. I am a heliophile and harbour a strong desire to stay where it's hot, therefore being a ski-instructor will never give me that warm feeling of excitement in my belly. I also happen to be a night flower and blossom in the midnight light. I won't be developing a love affair with early rising any time soon. As such, accepting a job that required me to be roaring to go each morning at 6am would be denying what makes me happy *and* when I am at my most productive. Remember the old saying, the truth will set you free? Be true to yourself and don't be scared to articulate what you crave.

There's also the question of being honest with other people. Admit what you really need *and* ask for it. Boundaries tell those around us what is and isn't OK. It is often the case that we internalise our boundaries expecting people to be clairvoyants. Then, we reprimand them when they violate these terms, which were only known to us. You can't be upset with someone for disregarding your truth if you don't speak it. If you don't ask, you don't get.

4.   Doing more of what we like and less of what we don't

Doing things you don't want to do is also a form of lying. You're saying you'd love to go somewhere when quite frankly you'd rather not. We expend a lot of our energy buying things we don't need with money we don't have to impress people we care little for in places we don't want to go to. Nothing emphasises this fact quite like *The Life-changing Magic of Not Giving a F*ck* by Sarah Knight (2015). In the book, Knight schools us against spending time that we don't have with people we don't want to spend time with, doing things that we don't want to be doing either. She urges you to be strict with your energy budget: if it doesn't make you happy, then you can't afford it. This is a very important part of unburdening yourself from social convention because trouble arises when you stifle your own needs to please others. If you aren't fond of baby showers, bachelor parties or work functions, stop going to them. Life is too short to spend time doing things you don't want to be doing. It's really that simple. If today was going to be the last day of your life, would you choose to do said activity? If you took a life-audit, how much time do you think you spend doing things you like and things you don't like? The answer might hold a lot of insight into your current satisfaction levels.

You don't have to be busy all the time. It's OK to say no to social engagements. Certain social appointments just become part of the long list of life admin. Create a filing system of what is actually useful for you so you have the mental capacity to focus on what's actually important. Have a look at your calendar and cancel things you're not excited about. Replace the fear of missing out with the joy of missing out to reclaim your most precious resource: time. Don't let other people schedule your life or spread yourself too thin. Social fatigue is among the perils of keeping up appearances. When we stop spending time, money and resources on things we find irksome, we have more time to spend on the things we actually do enjoy and that tickle our fancy. We say yes to life and to having more headspace for ourselves. We're granted respite from the breathless and guilt-laden need to be constantly productive and useful. Stop doing what you think you're "supposed to" be doing or what is polite. Accepting every request that comes our way makes us perpetually busy. One may have a propensity to say yes if they are confrontation-averse. Saying yes against our will is approval-seeking behaviour, which can be detrimental to one's sanity. Change the way you view requests. Simplify your life by learning how to say no; don't be afraid to disappoint people. If you can't meet someone's expectations and need to take care of yourself, tell them. It's OK for your needs to come first. You won't make a ton of friends by being honest, but it'll get you the right ones.

You can enjoy most things in life if you decide resolutely that you will, *particularly* if they are things that *you* wish to be doing. Learn to devote more time to the things that inspire you than to the things that drain your energy. Beat to the sound of your own drum. If you wish to learn a new language, head to the nearest free language swap evening in your area. If you'd like to pick up a new skill, spend an afternoon at a bookstore reading through the literature. If you'd like to get fit, join a class. I implore you to do more of the things you enjoy. Distinguish what's important to you and do away with the rest. You can't please everyone, but you can certainly titillate yourself.

5. Differentiating between our wants and needs
This subtitle of this book is "Realise, Accept and Pursue What You *Desire*" and not "Realise, Accept and Pursue What You *Want*" for a reason. Wants are fleeting and can

be augmented by the way the wind blows. Desire is tied in with devotion, passion, yearning and eagerness; want is linked to preference, fancy, choice and appetite. You want things you like; you need things you desire. It's a hankering; it comes from your soul. The things you need are the ones that are *essential* for your survival and happiness.

The study of happiness is far from the road less travelled in contemporary psychology. From the scholars and philosophers of yesteryear to today's positive psychologists, happiness, its meaning and pursuit have been extensively dissected and discussed. While many disagree with looking for happiness, others insist that we cannot take a passive approach to how happy we feel. In Mihaly Csikszentmihalyi's groundbreaking offering, *Flow: The Classic Work on How to Achieve Happiness* (2002, p. 2), he asserts that "happiness, in fact, is a condition that must be prepared for, cultivated and defended privately by each person". He reminds us of Aristotle's contentions regarding happiness: "While happiness itself is sought for its own sake, every other goal - health, beauty, money or power - is valued only because we expect it will make us happy" (p. 1). If being happy is a universal aching, what then, does it mean to be happy? Philosopher and historian Jennifer Hecht offers an answer and proposes that there are three types of happiness: Good-day Happiness, Euphoria and A Happy Life. The first set covers the things a person needs to make a good day for them. These could include seeing friends, chatting with neighbours, playing with your children, reading a book, playing a game or taking a walk.

The next form, Euphoria, is attained through activities such as meditation, crowd celebration, music, dance, art, deep laughter and adrenaline sports. The third type, A Happy Life, encompasses the things one feels they *need* to have or be working towards in order to like their lives. This includes family, friendship, travel, skills mastered, celebrations and rituals, money in the bank, community service, adventure, serving as an inspiration, a history of *some* euphoria and a history of *a lot of* good days (Hecht, 2008). A straightforward means of understanding happiness in terms of our needs and wants comes from author Will Bowen's offering, *Happy This Year* (Bowen, 2003, p. xviii). In his estimations, "happiness is the beach. Joy is the waves. Happiness is an emotional foundation of our lives, whereas joy ebbs and flows and is dependent on what occurs in our lives". Here we may view the things we *need* as happiness giving and the things we *want* as providers of swaying moments of joy.

You can indeed want something without needing it, that's the difference between adults and children. Kids think they need everything and will cry till the cows come home until they get it. A few years ago, my 2-year-old niece threw a tantrum at my mother's birthday lunch because she wanted to cut the cake herself and dig right in. We told her that she couldn't because it wasn't her birthday this time, so it was someone else's turn to cut the cake. She was having none of it. She screamed at the top of her voice and said, "But I need it. I need the cake". We all know she didn't actually need the cake, but rather, really, really wanted some. You may want some cake, but you'll be just fine without it. As many of us express who we are based on our consumption identity, it is commonplace to want things we think we are "supposed to have": nice cars, flashy clothes, expensive vacations etc. I wanted a promotion at my job at The Agency because I was "supposed to" get one after working there for a specific period of time and getting one would signal that I was appreciated and thus successful; ultimately, for ego-related reasons. So I wanted a promotion, but did I really need the extra hours and elevated stress?

If you categorise the wants as simply nice-to-haves, then you can better focus on your needs. You might want chocolate right now, but you need food to survive. You may want a beach house with a balcony, but you need a roof over your head to shelter from the storm. You could want to be slim and muscular, but you need a healthy body. You want people around you, but you need good, loyal friends. You want a drone but you just need a camera to preserve your travel memories. It helps you put things into perspective. Often when you say you need something, you really just mean that you want it. Like when you say you need the new Awesome Phone GX6 when you just got the GX5 eight months ago. The GX6 has a flashier camera and a better gyroscope, but do you even know what a gyroscope does? The old model never stopped making calls, sending texts (that bygone pastime) or Instagramming sufficiently, so did you *need* the GX6 or did you just *want* the GX6? Our lives are filled with so much clutter; things we have amassed because we "needed" them, but actually very little is *essential* for your happiness and contentment.

6. Worrying less

Children are jovial because they don't have a file in their minds called "all the things that could go wrong". We adults, however, seem to love that file and carry it around with us wherever we go, downloading new material and data to back up our unease. You'd be astonished to realise how much time we waste going back and forth in our minds, raging a war within ourselves. The fact that we as humans are cognitive beings is our greatest strength and also our greatest weakness. If we let ourselves, we could spend every waking moment disquieted. On a macro level, there are wars, famine, poverty and sickness. What are we going to do about it? On a personal level, there are bills to pay and errands to run. When will we manage to do it all? There are numerous reasons why we over-think and worry excessively. We have personal standards we wish to meet and things that are expected of us by others. All this sounds a bit boring, doesn't it? There are a gazillion much more fascinating uses for your headspace than worrying; it's totally a waste of your creative potential. Why worry about banal things you can't control when you could dream of unicorns or being handed a gold medal by Charlie Chaplin? Why worry at all? If you're worried about a problem, you duplicate it by adding worrying to your list of preoccupations; yet another problem is created. What will be will be, just relax.

Worry and over-thinking affect your sleep and your composure; they are the principal sponsors of sleepless nights. What do you tend to worry about the most? What keeps you up at night? It is within our own power to guide our thinking. Worry and self-distrust are learned behaviours and therefore can also be unlearned. You can interrupt your distorted thinking by asking yourself what else you could be contemplating that might be more fruitful for you. Make yourself more aware of your thoughts and find coping mechanisms to deal with bad days. Also, remember that bad days don't last. They can't. There are too many juicy things that are yet to come your way. Worrying means living with mental shackles. Free yourself from self-inflicted tyranny and silence your harsh inner critic. Get out of your head and get into the now. Being anxious and over-thinking removes us from the present; we're not really here, we're over there in the place where everything goes wrong. Worry less, live more in the now. Simple.

7. Living in the moment

Try to think about five of the happiest single moments of your life (hard isn't?). What do you remember about them? What was the common denominator amongst them? You were probably in the moment. You listened deeply and felt every sensation. More often than not, mine included music, friends and sunshine. One of them was dancing with my mum at my sister's wedding; I still remember the physical pain in my stomach from how hard we laughed. Another was on a sunset boat ride on the Pacific leaving from Honolulu's Waikiki Beach. It was the blissful way the wind caressed my face that has emblazoned this one into the vault of my best thoughts. Another was at an open-air Calvin Harris concert in London, long before his Taylor Swift days. I closed my eyes and I could almost feel the sounds pulsating through my blood. I opened them and I could almost see the smiles of my friends in slow motion. It was euphoric.

Bestowing sanctity on every act, no matter how big or small is what empowers us to enjoy life fully: every bite, every drop, and every ounce. Sacred is simply a means to describe that which is supreme, the utmost and the greatest: the greatest taste, the greatest intimacy, the greatest meaning, and the greatest ecstasy. Weaving the greatest appreciation into each act increases our enjoyment of it. There is so much to connect with every day. You can be excited about laughter, taking a bite, anything at all. Often, we find ourselves in an unproductive cycle of bothering about the future and chewing over the past. We habitually look at the past through glittery eyes, worry continuously about the future and as such completely bypass the present. In *The Happiness Makeover*, change expert M. J. Ryan goes as far as to propose that "happiness must be experienced in this moment or risk never being felt at all" (Ryan, 2008, p. 4). Our attempts to live "in the now" can significantly alleviate our suffering. In my book, *365 Ideas to Enjoy Your Life Today*, I outline a number of ways to help you live in the moment. Here are a few for your sampling pleasure.

1. Pretend tomorrow doesn't exist and is a utopian concept. If you are truly living for each set of 24 hours, what amazing things will you pack into them?
2. Make space for your future to make an appearance at its own time.
3. Live each day as if it were your last.
4. Disconnect from technology, the Internet and Social Media for a given portion of the day. If you can, switch off your phone for an entire evening.
5. Really notice what is happening around you right now.

6. Let yourself be bored. Spend a few minutes each day doing sweet nothing.
7. Lose track of time.
8. Look up at the way the light glistens through the water while you're taking a shower. Appreciate the majesty and tranquillity of water's flow.
9. Gaze at the sky and think about the shapes and colours of the clouds. Watch as they sway across regally.
10. Do one thing at a time. Give something your undivided attention.
11. Allow yourself some time to relax in bed before getting up.
12. Eat a whole meal in silence. Place all your focus on eating and doing nothing else.
13. Have a delicious stretch when you wake up in the morning. Have a good stretch standing or on the floor, in the morning or at night in bed. Your body will thank you for it.
14. To extend the enjoyment of your meal, fantasise about what your food will taste and feel like before it comes in contact with your mouth.
15. Smell things. So many rich scents and fragrances surround us, both natural and manmade. Walk past a bakery to get that fresh bread aroma, or stop and smell the flowers. It can be ever so therapeutic. Pause, smile and carry on.
16. Listen to your surroundings. There is a sound to breeze hitting leaves and birds chirping. We oft forget to listen to nature's music.
17. Take a walk under a deep blue sky and feel its tender warmth. Breathe in the delicious air, look above you and remember how great it is to be alive.
18. Enjoy the feeling of the clothes you wear and the cloths you cover yourself with.
19. Dance in front of the mirror.

20. Go towards the sunlight. Wherever you see a glimmer of sunshine, follow it. Walk on the sunnier side of the road and let the sunrays tickle you.

21. Feel every drop of water land on your head as you shower.

22. Take a deeper look. Zoom in closely. Our sight is our most used sense, but what are you actually seeing? Do you still notice the tiny details? Do you see the same things over and over again? Look at things with fresh eyes. Absolutely anything can be fascinating if looked at with a long, loving gaze. There is an abundance of great sensory details in even the smallest fragment. The eyes are the window to your soul; use them to see the beauty in front of you.

23. Enjoy the sound of someone's laughter.

24. Close your eyes and breathe in deeply. Count to ten and then exhale out loud. Repeat as often as you like.

25. Experience your surrounding environment without judging your thoughts.

It is how *well* we live which matters the most and not how long we live. We misguidedly play it safe because we think we have all the time in the world and that we can delay all our dreams until tomorrow, becoming masters of delayed gratification. It is courageous to address the elephant in the room which is that you don't actually have all the time in the world. You have today and you have now.

8. Holding on to our imagination

By now you would have noticed several analogies relating to children throughout these pages. Perhaps for lack of having the actual answers to life's questions, children let their imaginations guide them instead. They live colourful lives filled to the brim with playfulness and pure amusement. For them, life is one big open playing field of a dream.

Playfulness and humour

On the topic of playfulness, at one point or another, we are conditioned against possessing a comical disposition; we are "supposed to" grow up and get our act together. Society suppresses playfulness to the extent that many people can only let themselves go when inebriated or under the influence of some substance or another. When we were children, however, we had the freedom to play with our identities and we weren't preoccupied with the appropriate age to play with dolls or suck our thumbs. We were just beings. Free in our minds, free to play and free to be. Then we grew up and started to lose our neoteny. Adulthood beat the artistry out of us. In the midst of all our busyness, we minimised the importance of having pure unadulterated fun, life got so serious. Our society has no patience for adults who demonstrate juvenile characteristics (with the exception of actual comedians and clowns). There are set times for play. We are granted a few years from 0-12 and then our primary focus is to be shifted towards efficiency. Once our machines begin to run out of steam, we may once again resume play in our 60s. By this point, however, we've dedicated almost our entire lives to working - how will we even know how to play anymore? Will we have the energy? When we stop playing, we grow old in our minds. It is important to retain your childlike malleability and play throughout your life and not just after hours at bars, comedy clubs, the cinema, theme parks or any of those other places where grown-up play is "allowed".

You are allowed to have fun every day. You don't have to wait for those sacred holidays months from now, or even until the weekend. From the moment you get up, till the second you lay your head for slumber, you can add fun elements to each 24 hours, so it feels like every day *is* the weekend. Play can be seamlessly included in everything we do throughout our lifetime. For children, every day is a new adventure. They love to play and there is nothing to stop us adults joining in on the fun. You don't have to stop playing because society says it's time to get serious. This is by no means advocating eternal adolescence or living off the folks indefinitely. I'm referring to maintaining a healthy relationship with your inner child. We know that the necessity to play still exists, that's why events like the annual pillow fight in Manhattan's Washington Square Park is put on each spring (so much fun). It is our right to live pleasure-filled lives. I am not talking about erotic pleasure, gluttony or even lust either. I am alluding to the simple enjoyment of all that is undertaken: fun for no reason.

When we play, we enjoy our lives more (it's not rocket science) but also, we become more fun to be around. That's why playing games with children is so enjoyable. Why is my nephew Alex so charming? He's just a baby. Why does he disarm people instantly? Because he smiles with his eyes and his whole body, which trickles joy through every corner of my mind when I witness it. Kids don't take themselves too seriously either; they are bright flames yet to be confounded or put out.

So, how can you start playing again? Pull a silly face

unexpectedly when a friend is speaking to you. Wink at the next stranger that passes by. Wear your roommate or partner's clothes and wait to see their reaction. Inject a funny word into your sentence and see how long it takes for someone to notice. Great options include bumfuzzle, collywobbles, wabbit, lickety-split or nincompoop. Laugh and smile more. It might feel forced to laugh when you aren't in a great mood, but smiling can trick your brain into thinking you are, like some sort of groovy self-fulfilling prophecy. He who laughs lasts longest, so fake it till you make it. Nothing beats the feeling of deep breaths and a sore stomach after laughing hard. Life is better when you're chuckling. When was the last time you did something truly silly? When you felt like a playful kid again? Recognise that life is not meant to be taken too seriously. The reason you'd like to get back to *yourself*, your un-programmed Unconditioned Self is so you can enjoy your life, right? Well, playfulness and a sense of humour can help with that. They are two of the most valuable assets you can own.

Dreams and openness

Without hopes or dreams, life is a bird with broken wings that can't fly. A bird that is unable to do the very thing it was meant to do, sitting in a corner and merely existing. It is our thoughts that give us wings and our curiosity is the wind beneath them. When our imaginations are roaring and open, so too are possibilities; we believe in things so we ask for things for ourselves. The fact that children often choose being an astronaut as their dream profession summarises perfectly how far out toward the stars they shoot. They aren't worried about the fact their office will be on another planet. They aren't worried about the stiff competition. They aren't worried about rejection or danger. They aren't worried that they don't know what NASA stands for. They aren't bogged down by the details; they just have a dream. They enjoy the rose and don't preoccupy themselves with the thorns.

What I would like to discuss here are the sweet dreams we have can have while we're awake. Having a creatively vivid imagination means that you can conjure up any lifestyle for yourself. Being an artist is the best excuse for being eccentric, but if you think having a colourful imagination is solely reserved for the poets and painters, promote yourself to the resident artist of your life's project. Whether they sound crazy or not, shout with fervour all about your desires. Your dreams are yours to keep and no one else's.

Hoping and having dreams worth fulfilling make you feel alive. Strive to feel that way too. *Do* what makes you feel most alive. *Be* with people who make you feel the most alive. *Go* where you feel most alive. Shut your eyes and visualise your happy place or your paradise. How magical it is that we can be in two places at once. The beauty of dreaming is that there are no rules. Your inner child would never ask whether certain dreams were permitted or not. Think big. Hold onto your dreams even if they seem infantile, elaborate or difficult. Where would you live, what would you do, *how* would you live if there were no constraints - money, time etc? If you shake the dust off your book of dreams, I bet there are still a few sitting on the shelf. As long as you keep a little fire burning for your passions, you have the possibility of encountering magic. Let possibilities find you. They'll have an easier time locating your address if the doors to your heart and mind are open. Broaden your imagination and don't be afraid to grant yourself everything you ever hoped for in life.

9. Shifting from a scarcity mentality to an abundance mindset

Glass half empty, sourpuss, defeatist, killjoy, crepehanger: there are many labels for the scarcity mentality. If having a life filled with all your desires is what you're after, worrywart thinking won't afford you the pleasure, I'm afraid.

Optimism and positivity

Feeling good is natural. Feeling good feels so wonderful because it's inherent. We're meant to feel good. That's precisely why feeling bad is such an unpleasant sensation - because it's not natural for us. If falling sick after dining at a particular restaurant was a certainty, would you still decide to go in and eat there? Isn't going into any of your endeavours with a negative mindset reminiscent of walking into that restaurant? You know that putting on a negative thinking cap will never ensure a positive outcome. Ordering a meal from that menu of doom is the same as allowing negative thoughts to eat away at your fruitful harvest - you know it will contribute to your ill health.

Optimistic and pessimistic thinking each have their consequences. If you view your life negatively it will be just that - negative. If your input is exciting and encouraging, your output will be too. If the pictures you paint in your imagination are of unpleasantness, your life will be an exhibit of just that. You won't have a positive life with a negative mind as your thoughts paint your reality. Your thoughts become your words, your words become your actions, your actions become your habits, your habits become your values and your values become your future. If the input of all of these things is negative, the outcome will be too. We see what we choose to, so why not see beauty in everything? Pessimism and helplessness are a package deal. The mind is a particularly powerful instrument that can be used to leave us dejected *or* delighted. Through mere belief, we can think ourselves happier, more successful or whatever we hope for. Positive thinking lends us a cloak of protection in adverse times. Viewing life through an optimistic lens empowers us to better cope with setbacks, as at times, our optimism is greater than realism justifies. However, being optimistic isn't about being blindly unrealistic. Far from being a liability, optimism is an asset when managing our emotions. Optimism won't make your dilemmas disappear but it won't hurt you either. Think yourself *into* being happy, not out of it.

It's not uncommon for positive thinking to be lambasted as a means of living in La La Land forevermore, but true black is exceptionally rare. There are always lighter shades in dark colours. You will always be able to find light through your struggles. An abundance mindset is holding that glass up high and *believing* it's full. Cultivating a positive attitude means bringing your own sunshine wherever you go and choosing to look on the bright side, it's a choice. You can opt to see beauty in everything because there *is* beauty in everything. Even faded, brown roses are beautiful. Every day *could* be the most beautiful one of your life if you let it.

Shift from a scarcity mentality to an abundance mindset by practicing positive thinking. Positive visualisation goes a long way to assist with this. Create a mood board; find images of things that resonate with you, places you envisage yourself, things that make your heart tingle, or magazine cut outs. Plaster them in a book, at your desk, on a wall, by your bedside table or as your screensaver. Visualise yourself as happy. Sustain an outlook that the best is yet to come. There are so many things to look forward to: dreams not yet dreamt, friends not yet met, magic still unknown. Watch the impact on your attitude if you try to go a whole day without complaining once or saying, "I cannot", "I dislike" and "I hate". Choosing to view life positively sets us free to pursue our hopes and rise to the occasion that life is.

Gratitude

An abundance mindset will take you much further than being a doubting Thomas. The easiest way to abandon a scarcity mentality moving forward is through gratitude. Being grateful makes the world your oyster; it's the gift that keeps on giving. If you don't already feel fortunate and grateful for the things you have now, what makes you think you'll feel grateful when you have much more? Gratitude is being aware of the brevity of life and marvelling at its many splendours. Gratitude prohibits us from feeling sorry for ourselves. Gratitude is counting our rainbows and not only our thunderstorms. Gratitude is a safeguard against negative thinking.

There are a million and one things we could be grateful for, little and big: catching a whiff of a cake baking, sunny days, spring flowers, so-bad-yet-so-good TV shows, good books, your family and friends, a good night's sleep, good health, public holidays, blue skies, the stars, the sea, your favourite food, ice-cream, train travel, access to clean water. The list goes on. I personally am grateful for my sister, my brothers, the many people I have been lucky enough to call my friends, my background, my freckles (that I used to hate), the fact that beaches exist, that feeling of excitement just before I buy a plane ticket, and even avocados. I am thankful for the experiences I have with powerfully poignant music. I am grateful that sometimes a great song touches my ears and I get lost abundantly within it. I'm thankful that I am comfortable spending time in my own company. I am grateful for the preciousness of hugs that go on for about 11 seconds too long. I am thankful for the feeling of bliss when I eat something I like and the flavours explode joyfully onto my taste buds. My favourite Roquefort cheeseburger at a restaurant near my best friend's apartment in Paris has this effect on me; it's nearly beatific. I am grateful for a great many things. What are *you* grateful for? How can you practice gratitude? Before you go to bed, write down three things you feel cheerful about. Make an active decision to love the things you have, even if you can't have what you love. It is not happy people who feel gratitude, but grateful people who are happy. They say gratitude is the wine of the soul, time to drink up.

10. Owning our achievements

If you were asked to name five reasons why you dislike Paris Hilton at least one of them would probably be her sense of entitlement. It might be the fact that she's a "rich bitch" that seems to just sail through life (on yachts) without a care in the world, devouring designer handbags and expensive hair extensions along the way. But Paris Hilton is unapologetically Paris Hilton about everything. Despite years of ridicule, she continues with her "that's hot" catchphrase and very long blond hair extensions. The truth is, it really is hot that she's proven her critics wrong, re-branded herself time and time again and built an empire of her own. Ironically, the same society that encourages us to chase wealth and success knocks us down for it when we wish to enjoy the spoils.

Many a time we are scared of claiming our accomplishments because we're worried about the meaning of doing so. It may be insensitive to others or we don't think people will be genuinely happy for us. No one wants to be *that* bragging spoilt brat so you might be reluctant to share your happy news and experiences for fear of being boastful or arrogant. This creates what I can only call "happiness guilt" where we feel shameful about our good fortune. Why though would we ever feel guilty about the things we desire and had the strength, foresight and capability to manifest into our lives? It's fine to congratulate yourself especially if you've worked hard to get where you are. Why not shout from the rooftops about your accomplishments? Scared people will get jealous? Let them. Worry people will think you don't deserve it? Who cares if *you* know you deserve it?

In *Sex & The City*, there's a storyline that reflects this perfectly. Carrie dates the much-loathed Jack Berger in season six, a fellow writer. She receives a sizeable cheque from her publisher while Berger's recently released novel is tanking. Carrie is made to feel astronomically guilty about spending her money (and having it at all) because *he* doesn't feel good about *his* situation. While everyone gets envious, the people who truly care about your happiness view your triumphs as their triumphs too. It is asinine to fake humility to benefit other people's insecurities. Don't let fear of judgment from others stop you from being proud of your accomplishments and don't thwart compliments either. Respond with sincere gratitude, not false modesty.

A girlfriend of mine who worked at Google told me about how she suffered from Imposter Syndrome. This psychological phenomenon exposes unworthiness around success, a feeling that one is a failure despite evidence to the contrary. She felt she didn't deserve her prosperity and was a fraud that would sooner or later be "found out". In reality, she was more than qualified for the job and wouldn't have been hired in the first place if she wasn't. So, not much to find out then. Case closed. We can counter such doubting feelings by reminding ourselves of how far we've come and concurrently noting that it is not problematic to be proud of ourselves. You have more power than you realise; don't downplay it. Rather than waiting for someone else to do it, be your own full-time cheerleader. Become a professional in giving yourself motivational pep talks. You owe this to yourself for your efforts. You did the work; now get your bonus by depositing a wad of self-belief to your account.

11. Abandoning the search for perfection

Some people need pressure. Pressure *can be* of assistance to many. Some work better when they feel it while others can't handle even a whiff of a pressure cooker environment. Certain kinds of pressure serve the sole purpose of creating stress. The pressure to be perfect is one such example. One may strive to be the perfect mother, the model daughter or son, the perfect leader or the model citizen. By striving to be perfect, you make perfection the owner of your life. You become a servant to a hostile ruler that will never reward your efforts. It is a wholly unsatisfactory relationship, pushing water uphill without end. You might strive to be the top of the class, the best or the fastest in whichever race you're competing in, but what goes up must come down. Sooner or later someone else will be at your heels, desperate to take your crown. They'll go up on the leader board, as will your anxiety until you can take it back. Things that appear oppressively perfect are just that - oppressive.

What will really go wrong if you leave Pleasantville? Will the sky turn grey if things aren't perfect? No, it won't. Will everybody you have ever met in the world turn their backs on you if you take one wrong turn? I doubt it. Like the fear of failure, shame is at the root of perfectionism. There's no need to feel embarrassed about not being perfect though because nobody is. Detangle yourself from this idea that you need to be perfect because nothing is. There is no such thing. My perfect dream job at The Agency? Not so perfect after all. If you view something as being perfect it's going to be devastating if you happen to lose it. After all, how can you do better than perfect? Believing something is perfect makes it bigger and better than you and you may sacrifice yourself to keep it.

If you've been looking for perfection, call off the search party. Let your focus be on how far you've come, and not far how you have to go, evolution rather than perfection. You may not be the best, but there's nothing wrong with that. Striving to be perfect means you can't enjoy all the things you currently have and have done because you find fault and focus on what you don't have or haven't done. Perfectionism is a sinister creature and a deception at that. Striving to be perfect means you're still in competition mode, but in order to live *your* best life, there's nobody else in your category. It's just you.

12. Practicing feeling good

Feel-good mantras aren't only for hippy dippy spiritual tourists in Varanasi. You too can create your own mantras for serenity and personal growth right at home. Adjust your morning ceremony to incorporate mindfulness. Create a ceremony for you and you alone. When you wake up, decide one thing you would like to accomplish that day. This can give you a sense of purpose. It's OK if it's exactly the same as it was yesterday, but it provides you with something to work towards. Say an uplifting mantra out loud or recite an affirmation. Look at yourself in the mirror and declare your self-love and gratitude. Just like you'd practice the clarinet, practice feeling good. Tune your instruments to get the best sound out of your life music, whatever your preferred instruments are: yoga, meditation, swimming, running, faith or pottery. If the thing that gives you a pep in your step is a spritz of perfume, going for solitary walks, retail therapy, reading, dancing, cooking or binging on box sets, do it. Give yourself the gifts of the things you enjoy.

Have a range of feel-good exercises you use. Say "ha ha - hee hee - ho ho" out loud just for fun. Make cheerfulness a habit. Spend more time with people who cheer you up and remind you of your eternal loveliness. For some of us, contentment is a place. Wherever you feel good, that's where your place is. Your spot could be a specific park bench, your local bowling alley, the pier, the left side of your couch, your bed, under the shower, your office, the airport or your favourite café. Wherever it is, it's a place you can go for calm, to find inspiration, to think, to feel invigorated or just to be. After a while, this spot feels like home and you can take it with you wherever you go. Whenever you close your eyes, you'll be able to go there and feel just as calm and soothed. Claim it as yours and flee there as often as you can.

13. Taking action

Taking action requires clarity, choice and control. When you have clarity regarding your position, you can choose between many paths and aim to control the route your life goes along. There are many things you have zero control over in life, but your direction is not one of them. After all this self-exploration, do something about your realisations. It is an altogether more comfortable place being the writer of your own book, than the reader of your own book. You are the protagonist of your life story when you are comfortable with your choices and indeed act on them. If you keep thinking about things but never doing anything about them, life will feel complicated. Nothing will happen and you won't know why. Only action can initiate the changes you seek. Even starting off small is better than doing nothing at all. A tiny step in the right direction can end up being the biggest step of your lifetime. Take baby steps if you must, but do take the plunge. If you don't like where you are in life, move on. If you don't like the menu, leave the restaurant. If you're not enjoying the book, stop reading it. If you aren't enjoying the music, change the arrangement. Don't settle in this one life you have. You've got feet and can steer yourself wherever you choose. Instead of living a life that revolves around when next you can go on holiday, build a life you don't need to escape from. Escape permanently to your desired life. Dedicate yourself to seeing your dreams and goals through.

Taking control liberates and strengthens you. It gives you the feeling that things aren't happening *to* you, but *for* you. Taking control puts you in the driver's seat to pilot your own life story. Take control of your life, your finances, your friendships and your career because only you can steer them. And your plane? That would be your heart and your mind. It is never too late to take the reins and point your life in the direction you wish to take it. Octogenarians go on skydives and 9-year-olds write symphonies. It's absolutely never too late. Again, there is no hard and fast timeline for your life. Design what truly living means to you, map out your dreams and take action towards realising them. Don't coast along on autopilot playing a supporting role watching events play out with no input of your own. When you don't go after things, you don't get them.

Having clarity puts you in a stronger position to choose what's best for *your* life. You can choose to embrace your fears, get honest with yourself and other people, do more of the things you enjoy, worry less, live in the moment, retain the magic of your imagination, believe the glass is half full rather than half empty, to be proud of yourself for who and where you are without needing to be perfect. You can work to control the direction your life goes and put your choices into action. *You* are the most qualified pilot for the job. Take the route that answers the question of what *you* desire.

CHAPTER TEN
THE THINGS THAT WE ARE TO DECIDE FOR OURSELVES

You made it this far. You didn't stop reading when you were urged to think about some dark corners of your past, the failures and cherished components lost forever. You didn't stop perusing these pages when you were compelled to think about your fears and how you could overcome them. You persevered possibly because you wish to find out what happens to the protagonist at the end of the story. The protagonist here is you by the way. This chapter explores the certain decisions we are to come to on our own in order to be our true selves. Case in point, only you can know how good it feels to love what you love. Nobody can tell you who to marry (if anyone at all). Are you walking up the aisle because you're the last person in your circle of friends who remains unwed or your family is pressurising you to do so? If you aren't quite ready to say goodbye to the single life, the thought of begrudgingly buying anniversary gifts for the next 20 years will appeal to you about as much as eating week-old socks. Nobody can tell you what career you must follow either - not even a guidance counsellor. From a family of surgeons and expected to follow the same path but you happen to get squeamish around blood? Dear surgeon, if this isn't truly what you need out of life, each time you scrub up will be a grave encounter. There are certain decisions only *you* can make and some things only *you* can know about your life. These include the values and goals which influence the direction you take.

Who are you? (Values)

At the root of reclaiming your life is defining what *your* life means. The most rewarding pleasures are the ones which afford us a sense of meaning and purpose. Without meaning what's the point of anything? To borrow psychologist and writer Maria Konnikova's words, "It's the oldest story ever told. The story of belief - of the basic, irresistible, universal human need to believe in something that gives life meaning, something that reaffirms our view of ourselves, the world, and our place in it" (Konnikova, 2016, p.5). Having a purpose gives our lives direction and context. With purpose comes clarity. Your values are essentially your why and your how; your *personal* rules that *you* choose to live life according to. They affect your behaviour and help inform your choices. Having a third dimension to your life (spirituality, wellbeing, philanthropic causes, something other than career or home) can add a feel-good bonus to your life. Our satisfaction levels are significantly impacted by the absence and presence of aspects that are in line with our beliefs. I was hopeless working at The Agency because my work did not meet my standards of purpose. Whereas you might start off your career being motivated by making money, along the way your focus might switch to something else, perhaps giving back or work-life balance (as was the case with me). Values are stable but not static; discovering them is a process, that's why it's in our best interest to check in on them periodically. Defining your values simply means outlining what's genuinely important for *you*.

The decision of who you wish to be is yours to make and

yours only. Things that are fundamental to your very being - nobody else's hands belong here, poking and prodding away. This includes your faith, religion, lack thereof, your decision to be a vegetarian, to shun capitalism, to recycle, to solely eat raw food, to be polyamorous, to be celibate, to take a vow of silence, to live abroad, to live alone, to get pregnant, to adopt a child, to care for a pet, to study, to change careers, or to protest. Nobody else can understand the satisfaction and exhilaration you derive from these actions, so they have no authority to lord alternate choices over you. Only you can define who you are. We are told a great many things about who "we" are based on our race, nationality, gender, socio-economic status, family and religion. There are countless collective thought-processes that society encourages us to subscribe to but it is of utmost importance that *you* decide what your values are and that they are not thrust upon you. You are not your best friend, your neighbour, or your sister; you are different people. You are not living for them; you are living for yourself. You can chart your own path; you don't have to live, love, work or play like anyone else. When you are firm in your belief system, comparing yourself with others is less appealing because you simply don't share the same values. Knowing yourself inside out is key to freeing yourself from the traps of comparison-induced anxiety.

So it begs the question, what then are your values? What is your personal code of conduct? What do you stand for? What is important to you? What motivates you? What core beliefs represent your individual essence?

What is your life about? What brings you fulfilment? Think and answer honestly. Your fulfilment is contained within the answers to these questions. In my case, I enjoy travel so much because a life filled with adventure is something I value. Certain relationships have broken down because reliability and courtesy are also important to me. My close friendships are crucial components of my life because I believe in the healing power of community and connection. Wait no more, grab a pen and paper and start *your* list. As your collection of individual values starts to grow, place them into related groups. What are the themes that appear in your list? To illustrate, I hereby share some of the ideals that are of importance to me:

Community: compassion, connection, courtesy, empathy, fidelity, friendship, generosity, grace, harmony, love, loyalty, making a difference, mutual respect, openness, sensitivity, understanding, unity.

Adventure: curiosity, exploration, freedom, inquisitiveness, recreation, spontaneity.

Personal growth: competence, courage, creativity, development, flexibility, independence, intelligence, originality, passion, self-actualisation, self-care, self-reinvention, self-reliance, self-respect.

Positivity: amusement, cheerfulness, contentment, enjoyment, enthusiasm, excitement, fun, happiness, hope, imagination, inner harmony, inspiration, joy, playfulness, thankfulness.

Your values are revealed to you through the process of self-discovery. Use the information retrieved to figure out your framework in order to be able to play by your own rules. If you never think about *your own* principles, you'll vacillate between the ones handed down to you; you'll know only what you are "supposed to" value and "need".

<u>What do you really need out of life? (Goals)</u>
The question of what your goals are is a loaded and broad one. Sometimes the scariest part isn't working towards your goal, but admitting that it's an objective of yours in the first place. When asked the question "what do you hope for in life?" many will say they wish to be happy. Happiness is at the pinnacle of the personal goals of many, while others believe that its very pursuit guarantees that one never finds it. As previously mentioned, it is my personal belief that happiness can indeed be sought because we deserve to be happy. When you are open to things, they have a higher chance of coming into your life - and staying there. If you're looking for a new job, you open yourself to the new opportunity by applying or spreading the word among your network and updating your CV. Unless you happen to be lucky enough to get headhunted, a new job doesn't just fall on your lap. If you are looking to bolster your bank balance, you take the required steps to do so. You apply for a higher paying job, ask for a raise, start saving, invest or buy a lottery ticket (let's hope you don't go robbing any banks). Without these actions, the money simply won't fall from the sky; you'd need to take these first steps to manifest it into your life. Seeking happiness is simply *applying* the willingness to feel joyful. If we do

desire to feel happy about our lives, there are certain goals that have a higher likelihood of getting us there.

According to the Hedonic Treadmill (also known as Hedonic Adaptation), there are two types of goals: extrinsic and intrinsic. Extrinsic goals are targets like popularity, wealth, image, attractiveness and status. Intrinsic goals are inherently rewarding by themselves and are based on internal psychological needs that we share. These include but are not limited to personal growth, wanting to be loved, close friends, self-acceptance, affinity and contribution. These two value systems are somewhat paradoxical. We are happier in the long run when we focus on intrinsic goals as these pertain to our core desires and values. When we are motivated by intrinsic goals our actions *are* the outcome, not a means to an end i.e. to impress others, get rich. Pursuing extrinsic goals does not guarantee you happiness, because you'll never fully achieve them. There will always be more people to impress and more money to be made. Many of the wealthy industrialised nations with epidemic depression and anxiety are motivated by extrinsic values. Hedonic Adaptation means that we acclimatise to our situations, happiness fades and then we feel we need something else to pick ourselves back up again. It's an unending vicious circle for which relying more on intrinsic motivations is touted as an antidote.

It's important that your goals are guided by your values and not societal, age-related pressure points. Ambition and accomplishment may indeed be part of your dogma, but there is nowhere in the value system that says one is doomed if they have not become "successful" by the stroke of midnight on so and so date. We tend to impose stringent cut off dates on ourselves, but why? Because it's the "right" time? Because we "should"? Those timelines can feel like ticking time bombs. While that's all riveting and cute on Jack Bauer's *24*, that's no way to live in real life. Let's not imprison ourselves with strict deadlines. Being who you wish to be, doing what you wish to do with whom you wish to be doing it with may be implemented into every single one of your days. It's not a destination; it's a way of being. Dispose of the stopwatch and remember that this whole thing is about enjoying *your* life.

Breaking out of the box entails living and working towards goals that are based on *your* values and deep desires, and are consistent with your identity. The table on the following pages illustrates my goals that have been born out of my personal realisations and are informed by the things that are of value to me.

None of these goals have a time stamp. They are not goals regarding items I would like to own, but rather points to infuse into my way of being and what I would like my life to be comprised of. Living according to value-driven goals solidifies your getaway from living within the box along the yellow brick road, as they are deeply personal. While inscribing *your* goals, think about why you are on this journey of life. Where are you going? Do you like where you are? Do you like *who* you are? Is this what the rest of your life will be like? Would you feel proud of this? Find what's accurate for you.

Realisation	Value	Goal
I was relying on borrowed wisdom regarding how to live my life.	Personal growth/ self-reliance	Prioritising my personal needs & what makes *me* feel alive.
Success meant I was "supposed to" want money & prestige.	Personal growth/ passion	To live according to my own definition of success: feeling passionate & taking pleasure in what I do.
Failure filled me with terror.	Personal growth/ development	To focus on what I may gain from trying something (new skills & confidence) rather than what may happen if I fail.
I have told myself many self-limiting stories.	Personal growth/ self-care	To encourage myself, be my number one cheerleader & abandon self-synthesised narratives of powerlessness.
Travelling reminds me of my purpose & brings out the best in me.	Personal growth/ self-care	To incorporate travel into my life in a real way.
I compared myself to others negatively as I seemed to be living in a different time zone.	Personal growth/ originality	To be the trailblazer of my own pursuits & set my own pace for my life.
Spending time on my own is far from boring & puts me in a reflective mood.	Personal growth/ intelligence	To regularly check in & learn about myself.

Realisation	Value	Goal
The rigid structure of the 9-5 made me feel suffocated.	Adventure /freedom	To make my own hours & be self-employed.
Work-life balance is important to me. My job at The Agency took much more from me than it gave.	Adventure/ recreation	My job will never be *all* of who I am, but rather a part of who I am.
I was unsatisfied with my life in London & sought escapism through distractions.	Adventure/ exploration	To live a life I don't need to escape from by imbibing it with my desires every day.
Loss & rejection have been significant setbacks for me.	Positivity/ thankfulness	Finding the silver linings in trying situations.
Majority of my friends are open people I have a lot of fun with.	Positivity/ cheerfulness	To continually to seek out people who give every day the chance to be beautiful.
I feel most at peace when I am by the water & in the tender warmth.	Positivity/ inner harmony	To situate myself in places that are compatible with my preferences.
I was disconnected from my job at The Agency & had a feeling of futility about my work.	Community/ making a difference	I strive to inspire, inform & entertain through my work writing.
My friends & family have been crucial parts of my life during the good & bad times.	Community/ connection	To nurture & build supporting relationships.

How will you measure them?
In Business Management terms, you'll hear that your goals need to be SMART (specific, measurable, achievable, relevant and time-bound). Who you wish to be and your core desires are matters of the heart, however, and not trade problems to be managed. The goals that inform your being can be evaluated by looking at how happy, fulfilled and proud of your life you are.

Step one, how happy are you? What is happiness for you? If it's freedom, how free do you feel? If it's stability, how stable and secure do you feel? If it's close friends, family and community, how's your support network? If it's meaningful work, how pleased are you with what you do?

Step two, how fulfilled do you feel? The Cambridge dictionary defines fulfilment as "a feeling of pleasure because you are getting what you want from life" (Cambridge, 2018). We all have different ways of garnering these feelings of accomplishment and long-term contentment. Does the path you are on feel right? Personal fulfilment is your level of satisfaction based on your individual concept of life's meaning.

Step three, how proud of your life do you feel? I don't mean how much better is your life than someone else's. I am referring to dignity, honour and self-love. Do you accept who you are? Do you have remorse? Would you feel regretful if you left this earth tomorrow? Can you pat yourself on the back for the things you have done for yourself? What's your legacy? What will you be remembered for?

<u>What's your signature?</u>

At the end of your life, it will matter little that you were always the first one in the office, the best salesman or the youngest senior executive the company ever had. It won't matter one iota that you had millions in the bank because you can't take it with you. At your eulogy, no one will say how great it was that you did everything you were "supposed to" do before you hit 30. They'll talk about how you made them feel and how caring you were and come that day, you'll be able to know you lived your life to the full because you did it your way.

To help you action your goals, they may be condensed into a one-sentence guidepost for living wholeheartedly in your own way, as your true self. Call it a mission statement, your truth or a catchphrase if you will. I like to call it a *purpose declaration*. Unlike the resolutions you make (and forget) at the start of the New Year, this is an overarching motto and promise to yourself, a desire and a plan all in one. You may look to history's pioneers and dreamers to inspire your pen and create your own words to live by. Richard Branson's is "to have fun in my journey through life and learn from my mistakes". Maya Angelou stated that her mission in life was "not merely to survive, but to thrive; and to do so with some passion, some compassion, some humour, and some style". New American British princess, The Duchess of Sussex Meghan Markle has one too. "Always be true to yourself and be kind to everyone". And mine?

To fervently pursue exhilaration and adventure no matter what, and be an instigator of positive warmth in the world.

The "no matter what" represents a defiance against external bids for my compliance. My philosophy is simple. If it brings me a feeling of community and connection with others I care for, my answer is yes. If it taps into my need for exploration and freedom, I'm all for it. If it can help me grow personally, sign me up. If there's a glass there, it might as well be half full. These things fit into my *purpose declaration*. What's yours? If you were to conjure one up, how would it go? Better still than borrowing from others' purpose declarations, look to your own life and the realisations to be found from your varying facets. Your *purpose declaration* is an avowal which helps all else fall into place; it spurs you on to live in accordance with your principles. My premier ambition is to feel good and to utilise every moment I'm here to do so. While this may sound self-indulgent, at my eulogy someone might say "that girl, she really enjoyed her life" and they'd be right.

Escape to yourself

I urge you to upon reading this lifestyle design memoir and ode to free will, that you will think deeply about your own definitions of success and failure, your relationship with rejection and loss, your relationships in general, your recreation activities and the self-limiting stories you may have told yourself in the past.

I would love to share with you the realisation that there's nothing you "should" do because you're "supposed to". You can do only that which your innermost desires compel you to do. It probably also goes without saying that banning the word "should" from your vocabulary will probably do you a world of good, as previously indicated.

I would love to share with you the realisation that failing does not define you and in fact, can be a useful platform for learning. It is a showcase of your brilliance, resilience and courage.

I would love to share with you the realisation that while these experiences may be distressing, rejection and loss are not the end of the world. Your life can be counted in smiles and not only tears.

I would love to share with you the realisation that your relationships can speak volumes about what is important in your ecosystem and about your values. Spending time on your own is also an investment in your relationships as it teaches you more about yourself, your most important relationship.

I would love to share with you the realisation that one of the most powerful ways to get an education in the world and yourself is by travelling. Your cultural and personal understanding can be significantly bolstered by reading the pages of the world's book.

I would love to share with you the realisation that not everything that you tell yourself about your life is true. There are some half-truths nestled in there which unknowingly might have been keeping you stuck. These stories can also be re-written, re-jigged and sprinkled with new (rosier) information as you evolve.

I would like to bring to your attention the things you gain when you embrace change with open arms. You learn that derailed plans can sometimes be the most beautiful ones. You suffer less because you do not resist the inevitable and you make peace with the past. Life's unpredictability keeps things interesting, and change is at the heart of it.

I would like to bring to your attention the things you gain when you truly accept yourself. You harmonise better with people and don't reject love from others because you know you deserve it. You don't fight your emotions which means you are free to be you and you don't second-guess yourself. Your self-love is unconditional regardless of which tragedies befall you or which mistakes you make. You are one with your desires.

I would like to alert you to the steps you might take to set yourself free and move towards living according to your truth. Life is a journey in which you may take the scenic route to your destination via self-reflective practices, embracing your fears, being honest, doing more of the things you like, distinguishing between your needs and your wants, worrying less, living in the moment, retaining your imagination and positivity, owning your achievements, abandoning the idea of perfection, practicing feeling good and taking action.

I would like to alert you to the things you are to decide for yourself, the things only you can understand the true joy of: your desires, ideals, values and goals, for these are the building blocks of a life you can be proud of.

It is my wish that the three sections of this book have guided you to study the cards you've been dealt (realise), embrace the hands you've been given (accept) and play the game on your own terms (pursue). I hope you feel empowered to reclaim your direction because you are not tumbleweed drifting wherever the wind blows it. I hope you feel inspired to re-write the plot of your life if it stopped making sense and to ditch the script if you didn't write it. You're not living for anyone else and nobody's path is better for you than yours. Whether it's living by the beach or starting a family, get closer to your ideal life. You don't get a do-over. You might believe in the afterlife but you have no control over that. For all you know, you could be reincarnated as a dung beetle, so focus on the here and now. You have one life to live in a moment of an eternity, it's up to *you* to decide how you can love and live your life. So, have strange adventures, stay up late, dream awake, love hard, travel the world, breathe in, get lost, run, explore, go for midnight swims, make friends, ramble, laugh riotously, live a little. Be who you wish to be free of external blockades.

Escaping to yourself is a warm place because you accept and love yourself. For this reason, you gift yourself your heart's desires, only the best will do for you. Your life is a house that you can paint any colour and it needn't be in the shade of yellow brick road either. Go colour mad. Use reds and gold tones to orchestrate something brilliant. Feel free to colour outside the lines and break out of the box. When your days could be a soaring melody, a musical masterpiece, why choose a symphony in beige? You don't have to alter your life radically; you can just change the way you think about it. Your life is precious and therefore is best enjoyed the way you order it, not the way they want to make it. This is where my chapter ends; the next one is all yours.

REFERENCES

Introduction
- Bashford, S., 2017. It's a new dawn; it's a new day. *Psychologies Magazine*, January 2017, p. 27.

Chapter 1:
- Psychologies, 2015. The Fix. *Psychologies Magazine*, November 2015, p. 12.

- Holden, R., 2013. *Loveability: Knowing How to Love and be Loved*. London: Hay House, p. 20.

- Housden, R., 2005. *Seven Sins for a Life Worth Living*. New York: Harmony Books, p. 15.

Chapter 3:
- Lipsenthal, L., 2011. *Enjoy Every Sandwich: Living Each Day as if it Were Your Last*. New York: MJF Books.

- Brown, B., 2015. *Rising Strong*. London: Vermillion.

- Housden, R., 2005. *Seven Sins for a Life Worth Living*. New York: Harmony Books, p. 20.

Chapter 4
- Roberts, M., 2017. Fraught Festivities. *Psychologies Magazine*, January 2017, p. 42.

- Holden, R., 2013. *Loveability: Knowing How to Love and be Loved*. London: Hay House, p. 14.

- Chapman, G. 2015. *The Five Love Languages: The Secret to Love That Lasts*. Chicago: Northfield Publishing.

Chapter 5
- Housden, R., 2005. *Seven Sins for a Life Worth Living.* New York: Harmony Books, p. 14.

- Ferris, T., 2009. *The 4-Hour Workweek.* New York: Crown Publishers.

Chapter 8
- Edwards, G., 2006. *Wild Love.* London: Piatkus, p. 168.

- Holden, R., 2013. *Loveability: Knowing How to Love and be Loved.* London: Hay House, p. 49.

- Holden, R., 2013. *Loveability: Knowing How to Love and be Loved.* London: Hay House, p. 43.

Chapter 9
- Hecht, J. M., 2008. *The Happiness Myth: The Historical Antidote to What Isn't Working Today.* New York: Harper Collins, p. 21.

- Dimitri, F., 2015. School of Life Lessons. *Psychologies Magazine*, November 2015, p. 15.

- Knight, S., 2015. *The Life-changing Magic of Not Giving a F*ck.* London: Quercus.

- Csikszentmihalyi, M., 2002. *Flow: The Classic Work on How to Achieve Happiness.* London: Rider, p. 2.

- Csikszentmihalyi, M., 2002. *Flow: The Classic Work on How to Achieve Happiness.* London: Rider, p. 1.

- Hecht, J. M., 2008. *The Happiness Myth: The Historical Antidote to What Isn't Working Today.* New York: Harper Collins, p. 314.

- Bowen, W., 2003. *Happy This Year: The Secret to Getting Happy Once and For All.* Grand Haven: Brilliance Publishing, p. xviii.

- Ryan, M. J., 2014. *The Happiness Makeover: Teach Yourself to Enjoy Every Day.* San Francisco: Conari Press, p. 4.

- Bell, R., 2017. *365 Ideas to Enjoy Your Life Today.* N.P: Bell.

Chapter 10
- Konnikova, M., 2016. *The Confidence Game: The Psychology of The Con and Why We Fall For It Every Time.* Edinburgh: Canongate Books, p. 5.

- Fulfilment (2018). In: Cambridge Dictionary [online] Cambridge: Cambridge University Press. Available at https://dictionary.cambridge.org/dictionary/english/fulfilment [Accessed 24 May 2018]

ABOUT THE AUTHOR

Rosie Bell is an international travel writer, editor and author. Her notes on travel and lifestyle design have appeared in Forbes Travel Guide, BBC, NBC News, World Nomads and a legion of reputable publications on both sides of the Atlantic. Combining a background in psychology and communication with a career darting from country to country, she remains fascinated by the human condition and simple, inspirational ways to garnish it with love.